DIRECT SELL YOUR EBOOKS OFFLINE

Robert Stetson

DIRECT SELL YOUR EBOOKS OFFLINE
Copyright © 2013 by Robert Stetson
ALL RIGHTS RESERVED

TABLE OF CONTENTS

CHAPTER 1 THE CONCEPT 1

CHAPTER 2 PLAN THE BUSINESS 6

CHAPTER 3 FINDING DISTRIBUTORS 10

CHAPTER 4 TRACKING BOOKS 12

CHAPTER 5 WHILE YOU'RE AT IT 17

CHAPTER 6 EXPAND YOUR MARKET 21

CHAPTER 7 THE WEBSITE 24

CHAPTER 8 SELLING SOFTWARE 34

CHAPTER 9 A SELLING STRATEGY 39

CHAPTER 10 MANAGE PRICING 66

CHAPTER 11 MARKETING YOUR WARES 68

CHAPTER 12 DEALING WITH PIRACY 91

CHAPTER 13 THE MAILING LIST 109

CHAPTER 14 GOOD OLD EXCEL 110

CHAPTER 15 GETTING YOUR WEBSITE 111

CHAPTER 1 THE CONCEPT

The concept is simple. You have a nonexclusive license to sell your books and your software. Sell your eBooks offline and have the buyers download your books or your software from your own website. How do you do that? Simply market them at the local booksellers around town.

Let me make one thing clear. Selling your eBooks offline means "selling", not delivering. The delivery is done online.

It is possible to sell and deliver offline by having the book file on a media device and handing the book over to the customer on a CD at the time of sale.

If we look a bit deeper into the concept, you can offer the books or the software for sale with a split commission of anywhere from 50% to 75% for the bookstore. The online books on your website become inventory for the book seller.

Does 60% to 75% seem too high for the bookstore, just leaving you with 25% to 40% profit? Think again. Bookstores are considered "brick and mortar" retail outlets. That means they have to pay rent in order to stay in business.

Town taxes and employee payroll are an issue. While the online booksellers have the same employee payroll issues, the larger ones are usually selling many thousands of books per day, worldwide.

Protecting yourself and your inventory as well as tracking sales is easy, but you must have a system of checks and balances which are described in this book.

Are you tired of watching and waiting for your books to sell at the websites where you put them up for sale? Ever wish you could take an active role in getting sales by controlling the distribution? Ever wish you had an outlet for the nifty software that you have written? This book holds the solution.

This works for both software, eBooks and Paperbacks, but the eBooks and the software are far more difficult to control.

This book provides all the information you will need in order to establish your own private website for the sale and distribution of eBooks over the Internet.

Information is also provided enabling you to contact me in case you need assistance in accomplishing this goal.

There is a list of procedures you are advised to follow in the process of establishing your business and personal distribution channels.

If you're wondering why I have written this book, it's clear that there is enough out there for all of us.

I come from a long line of technical marketing experience. Competition is healthy. If you have an idea and no one ever heard of it, it can be the kiss of death.

In that spirit, you can also get this one rolling. You can collaborate with the little mom and pop bookstores in your area. It's risk free for them and for you. The eBooks take no inventory or shelf space.

Chapter 2 talks about the proper order of tasks and how to plan the business. It's important to identify your objectives before you begin, otherwise you get sidetracked.

Chapter 3 talks about how to develop your mom and pop book distributors. The goal is to put your ebooks books out for sale on the street. People will pay to download books if they know the bookstore they are dealing with.

Chapter 4 talks about how to approach the task of keeping track of your books and sales.

Also covered in Chapter 4 is the method of managing your accounts receivable and sales commission payment.

Chapter 5 talks about how to build on your inventory and product lines without losing sight of the main objective.

Chapter 6 talks about the best way to expand your market. Many businesses fail because they expand too soon or too fast. I will help you understand when the timing is right and how to do it without diluting your quality of service.

Chapter 7 talks about how to manage the sale of paperback books in the distributing environment along with your expanded offerings by way of your website.

Chapter 8 Gives you a method for selling the software you have created by way of the website and by way of your mom-and-pop connections.

Software sales can be made through the book distributors via links in your book.

Chapter 9. Sales Strategy 101. This section helps you set goals and shows you methods for meeting them.

Chapter 10 Pricing is store managed, but not always, and you need to keep an eye on cost versus revenues.

Many problems are addressed in this chapter to ensure that you are earning royalties fairly.

Chapter 11 Marketing your wares is not the same as sales strategies, where sales deal with the economics and marketing deals with the demographics.

Chapter 12 Dealing with piracy is something you have to come to terms with. This chapter tells you how to proceed when someone else is distributing your books without your permission, whether for free or for profit.

Chapter 13 The almighty mailing list of which there are two. The emailing list and the postal mailing list are not the same.

This recommends using caution around SPAMMING and Junk Mail.

Chapter 14 Good old Excel helps you put your business on paper so the computer is doing the math and tracking and you are free to just count your money.

Chapter 15 Explains how, you might be bewildered, but the idea of starting your own business is attractive.

I show you how to inexpensively get your website up and running with a minimum of time, effort and expense.

CHAPTER 2 PLAN THE BUSINESS

A man who stops advertising to save money is like a man who stops the clock to save time.
--Henry Ford

While you don't need a business loan to get this one off the ground, you do need a business plan. The easiest way to get help in drafting a business plan is to contact your local Chamber of Commerce and ask them about organizations that offer free help.

One such organization is the nonprofit called SCORE. It's over 50 years old and matches startups with volunteer mentors.

They are supported by the U.S. Small Business Administration (SBA) and has over 11,000 volunteers.

They have over 340 chapters holding events and workshops across the United States.

They are headquartered in Herndon, VA.

Be careful using these helpful resources because they can derail your activities with other planning.

I once started out to create a business and my mentors had me sitting in a corner day and night doing market research, writing a business plan and doing financial planning.

Every time I completed the task, they suggested a different way to organize the material and it was back to the business plan, which took forever because I had to do the new research. The market was changing.

After six years of good advice, I was still looking to start the business and knew all about it, but the market window had closed and it was no longer a profitable venture because I had failed to enter the market when it was time.

When you start a business everyone has advice for you. No one likes the way you plan to do it. Everyone knows a better way, but no one is stepping up to help. Ignore these people.

It's human nature to butt in. It's like when you buy something nice and suddenly everyone knows where you could have gotten one almost free. Why do people do that?

A business plan is not a business and it's not a product. You can't sell a business plan unless you need a loan or venture capital. I suggest you just dive right in. You can learn as you go.

Don't rent an office and don't hire employees. If there is something you need and you don't know how to do it, then hire a consultant by the hour.

Hourly consultants are the cheapest solution. When you develop your business, your done paying them. Do not take on a partner.

You don't need much if any money to get this thing in full swing. If it fails, you aren't out your life savings and you don't owe the bank.

When I say plan the business, I mean think ahead for what you need. Do not line up distributors until you have a product to sell.

Do not sign up for an Internet Provider until you have the HTML code written and the system in place. You don't have to be paying rent on an IP Address when you don't have a website yet.

You can buy a "cookie cutter" website and tracking system. I have one that I sell and it seems to cut a lot of corners for people starting out. This can minimize development time in getting to the profits and the bugs are shaken out already.

GETTING THIS THING GOING

The first order of business is to establish in your mind how many books you have to sell. The more books you have, the better positioned you are to make money.

Be careful who you deal with. Set the business up with your own books first and if you decide to bring on authors and their works, you would need a Lawyer and perhaps incorporate.

I advise against partners and authors riding on your business. They are an added burden and don't bring as much return as you would need to reap considering the amount of time and energy required to deal with them.

You will do best if you just consider this your magic nickel machine. If the nickels come fast and furious, and turn into mega-dollars, then maybe you can look at investing more time and planning.

I have a simple rule that tells me when to invest in my expanding business. If you're losing money by not having something, then buy it. If the item you're buying can't increase your income by more than it costs in the first three months, then wait.

Your book, book distributor, book customer and inventory tracking system are the first item on your list. Using a combination of Microsoft Excel and web page assignments, you can stay on top of these with minimal effort.

CHAPTER 3 FINDING DISTRIBUTORS

Approach the local mom and pop booksellers in your area.

A phone call can be beneficial in getting you a meeting with the store owner. Being on the phone with the owner is difficult because it seems like just another marketing scheme.

A letter is also a good way to start, but don't count on anyone answering it. In fact, many of the stores will throw an unsolicited letter or postcard away as junk mail.

Then there is the email telling them of your desire to meet with them and set something up as a potential distributor. This smacks of SPAM and people resent it.

Start by walking into the store and speaking face to face with the owner. This is done so seldom that the owner is more likely to talk to you, whether the outcome is positive or not.

Your job is to convince the local bookstores that people are buying eBooks now. This would be a good time for the bookstore to fight back by offering discounted books from their Sony, Kindle or e-book reader.

Brick and mortar bookstores are going away because of the eBook revolution. You can fight back by adding eBooks to your product offerings. Go with the flow.

Creating a mailing list of street addresses, phone numbers an mail addresses will serve two purposes.

It allows you to stop wasting time on people who don't want to hear from you anymore.

It allows you to forge ahead with sales activities where the people are receptive.

If things go well, the names can be transferred from the marketing list to the customer list.

Amazon has the right idea. Allowing people to simply return a book can save a lot of hassle. One has to wonder if arguing with a customer is worth the effort. I would let a customer return a book for a refund rather than argue.

When the customer returns two or more books, then I would go ahead and get aggravated with them. When a customer is stealing your book, then they are stealing your money.

I would allow the bookstore to work on the issue of refunds. In this way, the customer is not angry with me and I have not suffered any bad karma. Meanwhile, the bookstore is setting the standard for the return and is not aggravated with me.

As for me, I am pretty laid back and want to focus my energy on writing and running the book sales.

CHAPTER 4 TRACKING BOOKS

Each book in your inventory is equal in value to the money it represents. On the surface this seems absurdly obvious, but people often lose sight of the connection.

Each time you create a unique serial number, you create a physical book, even though it's an eBook file.

These basic serial numbers can be sub-serialized to allow unique book downloads. The unique books downloads will allow you to track individual sales by preventing the sale of the same serial number to more than one person.

Formats can be chosen to allow or disallow devices from being used. I have 4 formats. These are;

EPUB
MOBI
PDF
TEXT

The book serial numbers are printed onto tickets and the tickets are issued to the bookstore.

Do not sell eBooks in any format such as MS Word or you are inviting people to swap eBooks with one another. A single sale can disperse into hundreds in the underground trading marketplace.

When the bookstore issues payment via PayPal, the book is released for download.

Book purchases can also be made directly to you via PayPal by the customer who is then issued a book ID Number so they can download their books.

Title Code

The Rift	1173
Red Dwarf	1253
Red Dwarf II	1263
Red Dwarf III	1362
Red Dwarf IV	1433
The Book	1536
The Crucible	1537
The Crucible II	1625
The Crucible III	1635
Make Your Own Free Kindle Book Covers	1645
Make Your Paperback 4 Free	1746
Excel Course	5192
PowerPoint Course	1867
Mail Merge Course	1894
Electronic Business Cards	2736
How Disk Drives Work	2837
Impactful Marketing Under $10	3354
The Publisher's Microsoft Word Guide	4985
Software For Diabetics	1836
The Birthing	5264
The Cure	5345
Dark Star I	5554
Dark Star II	5937
Helloween	6354
Tablet PC Telephone	6374

Above is an example of a software download ticket issued to a customer for the purchase of the Excel Course program.

When the customer goes to http://WWW.RobStetson.com, they can click on the SOFTWARE DIRECT MENU button on the left side of the screen and enter the download process.

CHAPTER 5 WHILE YOU'RE AT IT

As you look at my website, notice that I have taken the opportunity to tout my classes and establish pages of my books.

This is not redundant, nor is it overkill. People who log on here for one thing might want to see what else I have available for them to purchase.

People who buy books might want to take one of my classes, so they can open the page and see what classes are available and where to call or email in order to sign up.

Folks who are taking classes may want to see what books I have written and where to buy them.

The presence of your books on the website are critical to your success. Taking a class from an instructor who has never published is like having a football coach who has never played football.

Your published works are your credibility. Make sure your books always are right out front.

DIRECT SELL YOUR EBOOKS OFFLINE

I don't go out of my way to sell offline to people who are visiting the site for a reason other than to buy books. For these people, the pages will link the interested person to my distributors and they can buy my books there.

DIRECT SELL YOUR EBOOKS OFFLINE

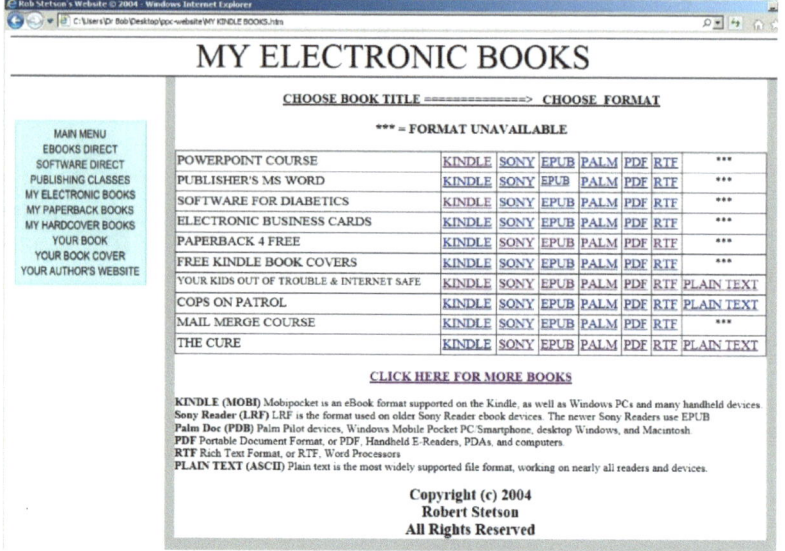

That is why the menu items "MY ELECTRONIC BOOKS", "MY PAPERBACK BOOKS", and "MY HARDCOVER BOOKS" are listed apart from the separate sales pages in "EBOOKS DIRECT" where prepaid customers paying through PayPal can then immediately download their product.

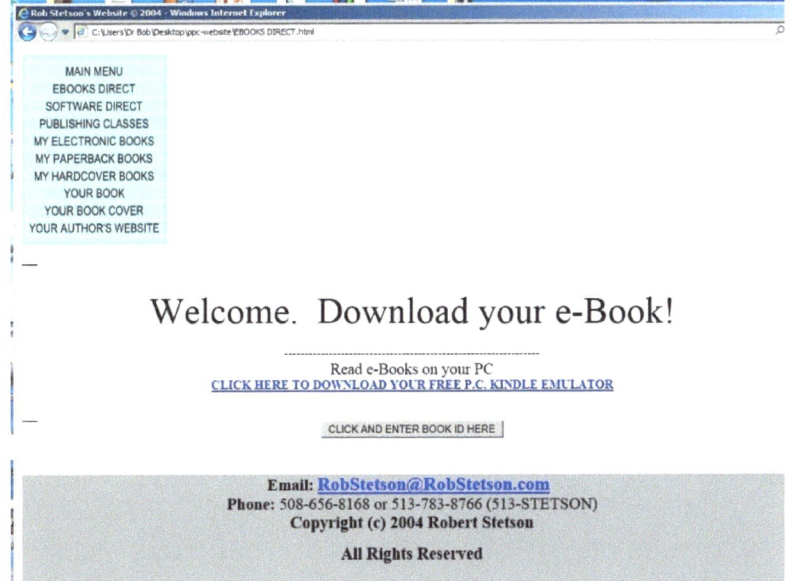

The "MY BOOKS" pages redirect the buyer to my distributors where they can place their orders and pay by credit card.

There is no point in selling paperbacks and hardcover books directly from your website.

The logistics are a nightmare. You have to stock the books, package them for mailing, travel to the post office or UPS and pay the postage. It's a lot of work and it will take you away from your business of writing.

CHAPTER 6 EXPAND YOUR MARKET

Selling your eBooks online through distributors is fine, but you can dramatically increase your income by having them sold locally.

Towns, schools and libraries are a good source of revenue for lecturing about writing, but your local bookstores need books to sell. The least risky book is one they do not have to buy until it's sold.

Consignment is a popular way to do business when you have copies of paperbacks or hardcover books.

The downside of selling paperbacks is that in order to have a book to sell, you have to buy a copy. The print on demand companies sell the books to the author at a deep discount.

The difference between the print on demand asking price, plus shipping and your retail price may not be as high as your royalty.

On the other hand, a sale on the open retail market is a sale that you would not have made.

DIRECT SELL YOUR EBOOKS OFFLINE

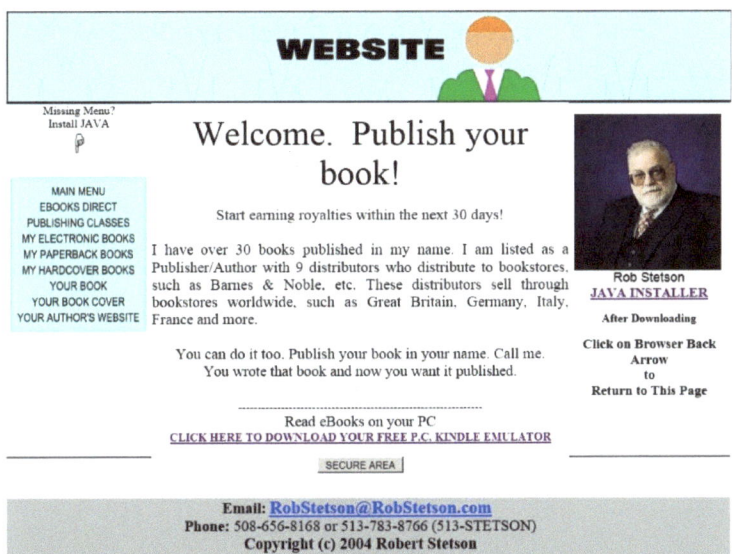

You might notice the use of secure area buttons all over the website. The buttons are linked to Java Script routines throughout the web pages and can easily protect areas from unauthorized access.

The Javascript routines have embedded filtering statements to prevent the entry of the wrong data field into the password key area.

The number 5192 can be used in the eBook section to access a book, but if the number 5192 is entered into the software section, the result will be very different, so the software program that is relevant to book number 5192 could be downloaded from the software download page. In this way the software code 5192 would be selected for download rather than the eBook using the same code.

If the number 5192 is entered into the Secure Access area, then it would be rejected, unless there is an access area code named 5192 associated with the ebook or the software.

CHAPTER 7 THE WEBSITE

The key to the success of this business is the software that controls and regulates the distribution of the inventory.

I have integrated the inventory control process into the website software. This will enable the exposure of the buying public to my website information while they are consummating their purchase from the bookstore.

There are two uniquely secure gateways in that entering the "Password Code" in the "Book ID Field" or entering the "Book ID Field" in the "Password Code" will not work due to the codeword filtering.

I have modified the password processing portion of the Java Script to attach a character at the end of the entry. The item being accessed must have a matching character in the name to correspond to the entry or the names will not match.

For this reason, when you enter a password such as "password" the filtering system attaches a "p" to modify the name to "passwordp" The password will not work in the Book ID Field because if you enter the name "password" in the Book ID Field, it will be changed to "Passwordh"

With the exception of these filters, the Java code is identical for both secure gateways. This gives the outward appearance of two distinctively separate coding systems.

The "secure area" button is for the retrieval of documents by students, such as handouts or course specific software. The "secure area" button is located on the opening page of the website. The "Book ID Field" is for downloading of books or product software.

This is a screenshot of the opening web page.

From this page you can download the Free Kindle Emulator application that enables you to read eBooks on your Microsoft Windows PC.

The second option is to click on the email link and send a message to the website owner.

The mouseover menus allow for changing from page to page, while the links and buttons direct you to other clearly defines areas of the website.

I have placed my bookstore download area at the top of the menu right under the "Main Menu" button. It presents itself to the purchaser of my books as the first option where they can download their merchandise immediately using the Book ID Code.

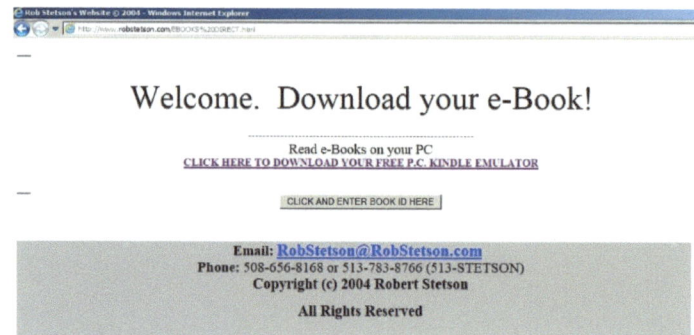

Clicking on EBOOKS DIRECT opens this page.

The eBooks Direct page is not the only page on the website without a Mouseover Menu. Using the back arrow on the browser will take you to the previous page, but otherwise the only option is to select one of the three other options.

From this page you can download the Free Kindle Emulator application that enables you to read eBooks on your Microsoft Windows PC.

The second option is to click on the email link and send a message to the website owner.

The third option is to click on the Button labeled CLICK AND ENTER BOOK ID HERE.

The Button links to the secure gateway as shown in the screenshot below.

DIRECT SELL YOUR EBOOKS OFFLINE

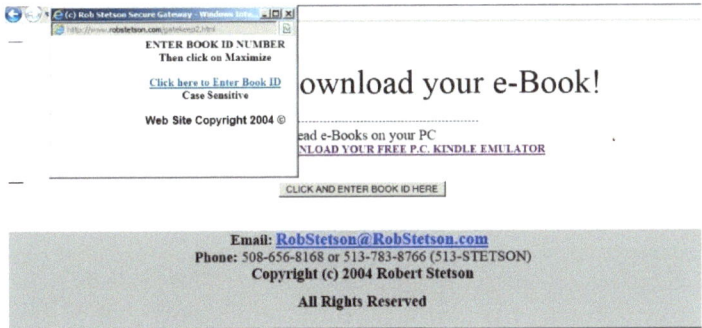

The user clicks on the link CLICK HERE TO ENTER THE BOOK ID.

This opens the Java Script Prompt for the Book ID Code as shown below.

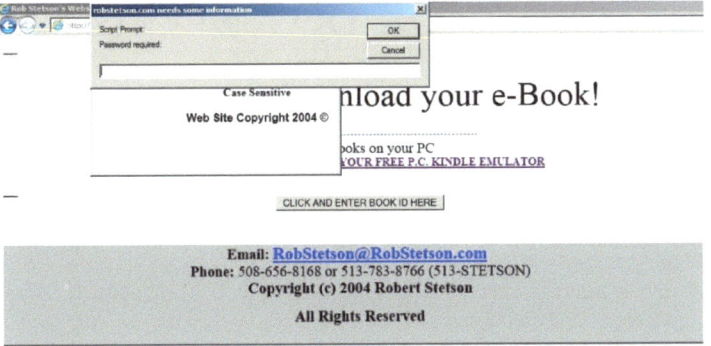

The user can enter their Book ID Number. Then the user connects to the document retrieval page for the book title selected.

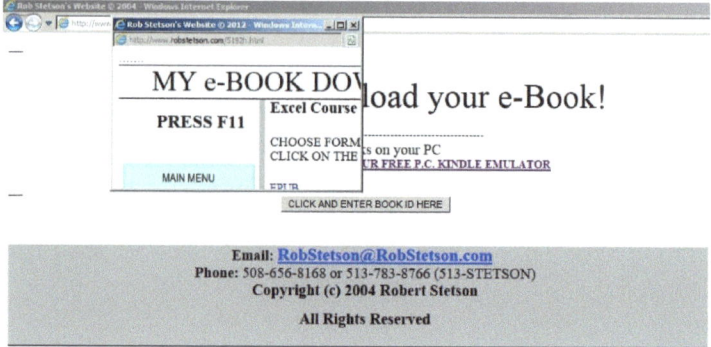

Once the correct Book ID Code is entered for (in this case) Excel Course, the window opens and instructs the user to press the F11 key.

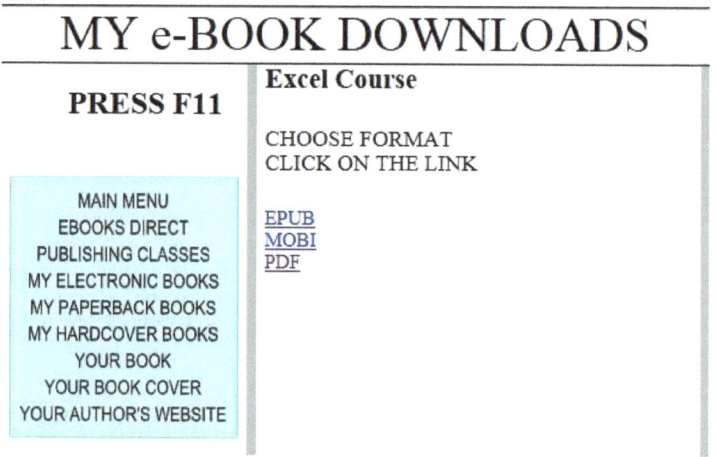

By clicking on EPUB, MOBI or PDF, the user selects their download format. The download will commence immediately. The book can then be read on the PC or your handheld device.

DIRECT SELL YOUR EBOOKS OFFLINE

Aside from the Mouseover menu option from the main screen, is the SECURE AREA button.

The Button allows the user to enter the password-protected area where special documents and specific software applications are downloaded.

DIRECT SELL YOUR EBOOKS OFFLINE

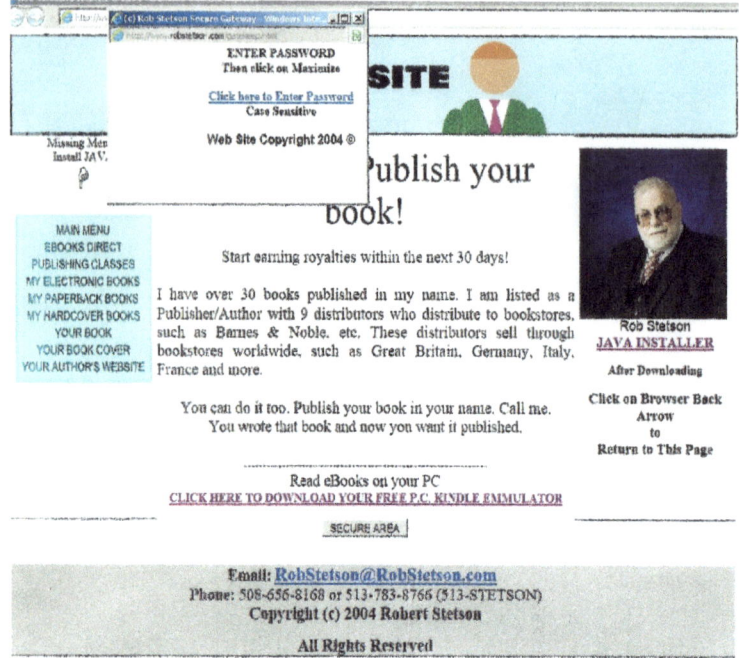

When the button is activated, the ENTER PASSWORD popup appears with a link to the gateway popup.

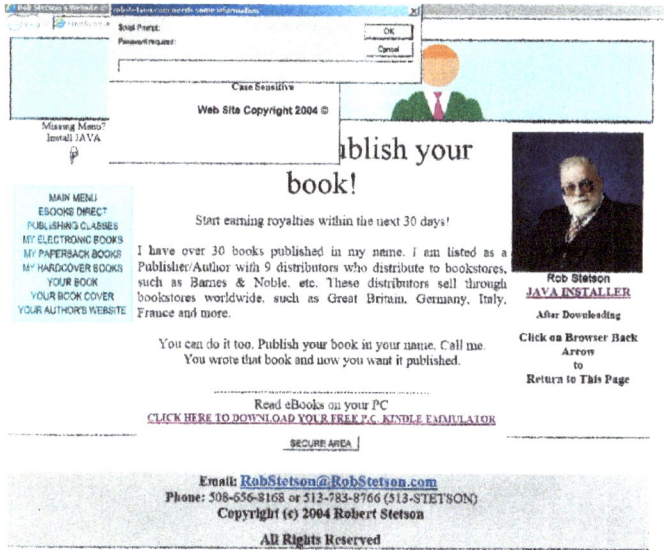

The password is entered into the Script Prompt and then the "OK" button is pressed. The correct password sends the user to the document or software retrieval page.

In this case, the document retrieval page offers the user a list of links that will enable the downloading of documents that are handouts for the two day publishing course.

The links on the CLASS HANDOUTS page offer three options. When the desired link is selected, the document immediately begins the download process.

DIRECT SELL YOUR EBOOKS OFFLINE

CHAPTER 8 SELLING SOFTWARE

Software is easily delivered using the Mouseover Menu as a vehicle to a secure area, just as the books are downloaded.

The coded software for this website is a perfect example of how the product can be sold and delivered.

Notice the addition of the "SOFTWARE DIRECT" button in the Mouseover Menu. You can add as many buttons of any kind, on any topic you choose. There is no limit to the number of keyword protected areas and items you are allowed to have.

Clicking on the SOFTWARE DIRECT button takes you to the

DIRECT SELL YOUR EBOOKS OFFLINE

```
MAIN MENU
EBOOKS DIRECT
SOFTWARE DIRECT
PUBLISHING CLASSES
MY ELECTRONIC BOOKS
MY PAPERBACK BOOKS
MY HARDCOVER BOOKS
YOUR BOOK
YOUR BOOK COVER
YOUR AUTHOR'S WEBSITE
```

Welcome. Download your Software!

[CLICK AND ENTER SOFTWARE ID HERE]

Email: RobStetson@RobStetson.com
Phone: 508-656-8168 or 513-783-8766 (513-STETSON)
Copyright (c) 2004 Robert Stetson
All Rights Reserved

Clicking on SOFTWARE DIRECT opens this page.

The Software Direct page is not the only page on the website without a Mouseover Menu. Using the back arrow on the browser will take you to the previous page, but otherwise the only option is to select one of the two other options.

One option is to click on the email link and send a message to the website owner.

The other option is to click on the Button labeled CLICK AND ENTER SOFTWARE ID HERE.

The Button links to the secure gateway as shown in the screenshot below.

DIRECT SELL YOUR EBOOKS OFFLINE

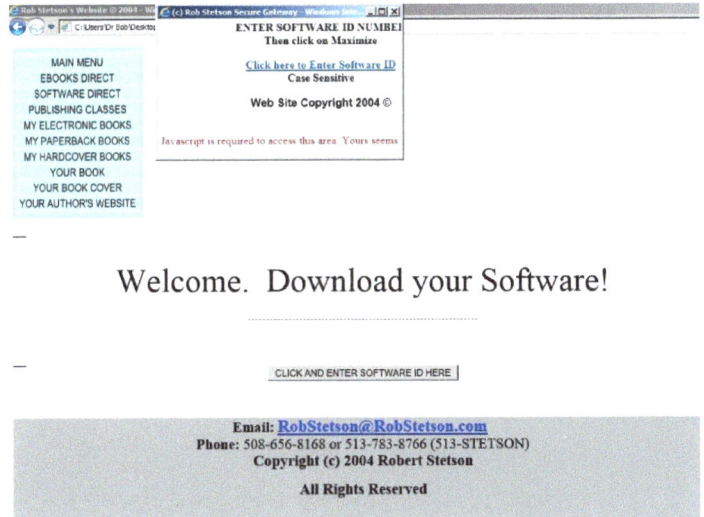

The user clicks on the link CLICK HERE TO ENTER THE SOFTWARE ID.

This opens the Java Script Prompt for the Software ID Code as shown below.

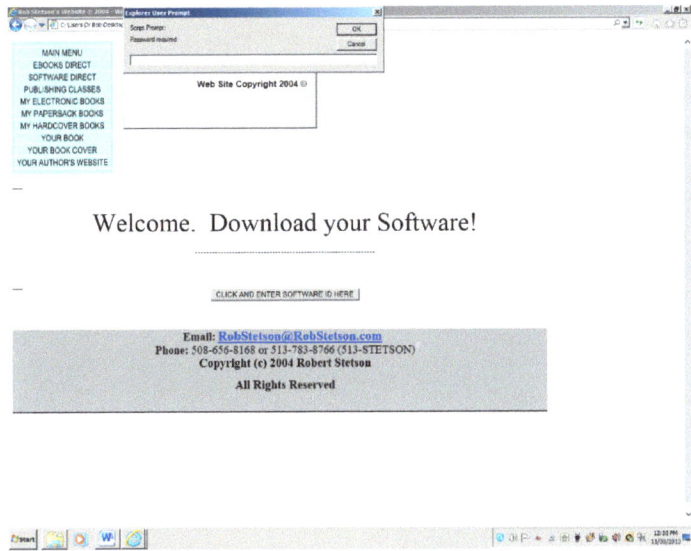

The user can enter their Software ID Number. Then the user connects to the software retrieval page for the software title selected.

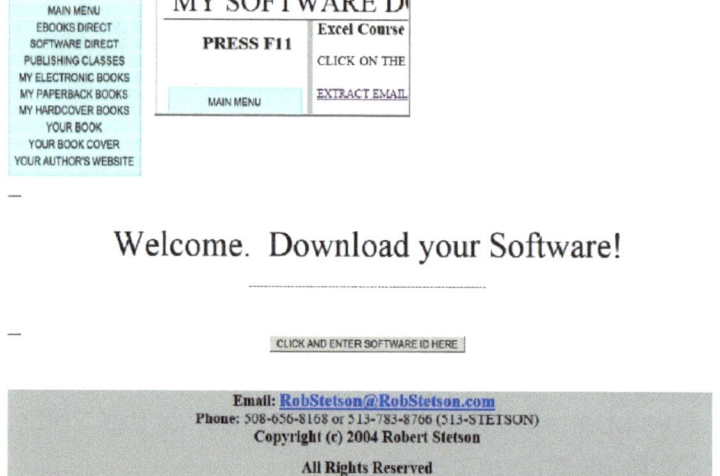

Once the correct Software ID Code is entered for (in this case) Email Extractor, the window opens and instructs the user to press the F11 key.

MY SOFTWARE DOWNLOADS

PRESS F11

MAIN MENU
EBOOKS DIRECT
SOFTWARE DIRECT
PUBLISHING CLASSES
MY ELECTRONIC BOOKS
MY PAPERBACK BOOKS
MY HARDCOVER BOOKS
YOUR BOOK
YOUR BOOK COVER
YOUR AUTHOR'S WEBSITE

Excel Course

CLICK ON THE LINK

EXTRACT EMAIL

The link named "EXTRACT EMAIL" is not a command link, but is the name of the program you want to download.

The program will download as a ZIP file. The download will commence immediately. The software can then be installed on the PC by extracting the contents of the folder.

CHAPTER 9 A SELLING STRATEGY

Once you have your website in place, you need to go to PayPal and open an account. The account is free and there is no charge for incoming payments from customers in the continental United States.

Incoming transactions from outside the Continental United States will generate a transfer fee, so plan accordingly when you price your books in Canada, Mexico or elsewhere around the globe.

You are now ready to create your local storefront distribution channels. Go online to Google and Yahoo to locate booksellers in your area.

Once you have established a few bookstores in your area, then you can branch out to other areas and spread as far and wide as you like.

I recommend that you not begin your sales activities outside of the distance you are willing to travel. Your first storefront distributors need to be close enough to visit for the face to face sales pitch.

Establish your business long enough to get comfortable with the flow of orders and redemptions. Sales support will require your personal attention, so be sure and be available for customers who are having problems.

Having a MagicJack phone is important so you can provide telephone support during normal business hours. The benefit of a separate MagicJack phone is that you won't be giving out your personal home phone. Do not use your cell phone for this purpose. It will only rack up hours on your mobile phone bill.

Don't let it get out of hand. The logistics of long distance business can be difficult when trying to track your sales in another city or state.

CATALOGS

The cover design is a critical marketing tool. I once had a book that languished for three months without a single sale. I changed the title and redid the cover and it became my hottest seller without any changes to the actual book content beginning the very next day.

> Maybe you can't **tell** a book by its cover.
> But
> You can surely **sell** a book by its cover.

Uploading Keywords and Metadata

No one can buy a book if they can't find it. Metadata is one of the least understood characteristics of your book upload.

There is more than one form of metadata. The definition of metadata varies, so we will define our terms here.

I regard metadata as the "search words" that are separated by comas (as a rule).

Words such as; action, adventure intrigue, mystery, romance, and others are usually used in this area.

These are the words that will draw people to your books and must be carefully chosen.

Finding your best keywords is something you should do before using them in your metadata.

Some people think these keywords include these data fields:

a. Title
b. Subtitle
c. Category
d. Description
e. Target audience

Figure out the keywords you most want to target.

Create a metadata master file in your MS Word or other program to hold your metadata.

The "description" field is the most important of all along with your "keyword list".

You have creative license regarding the content, so make it as compelling as possible. If the content of your exciting description is not exactly what the story is about, then either fix the description, or fix the story.

Nothing will alienate your readers as fast as a compelling description where the story falls short of the promise.

Don't do what the Hollywood movie crowd does. You see a preview and decide you have to see this movie; then the movie is nothing like the compelling preview, what a let down.

I like to write the description in a Word file and then a keyword list, then I cut and paste the content when I'm uploading the book to the website. It goes so much faster and I don't have to keep writing it over and over each time I upload to a different bookseller.

In case you never thought of it, I will jog your imagination here with the recommendation that you make a series of catalogs.

Nothing is inexpensive any more, but the catalog is something you can distribute and control.

Ink, especially color ink can make the catalog more costly to produce. You can prepare a text only catalog, but a book cover display in dazzling color can result in more sales.

More sales, in the beginning, might not be enough to offset the added pages and the cost of all that color ink. Also, you might try splitting the catalogs between fact and fiction.

I have included a couple of examples of catalogs showing the options. If you try and make a single all inclusive catalog, be sure and separate out the fiction from the factual book content. To combine them would make the catalog more difficult to navigate.

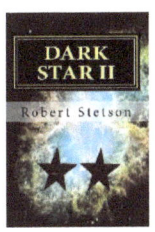

Dark Star, the invisible angel of justice. The Earth is ruled by a dictatorship by a One-World Dictator gone insane.

This is the story of the mysterious Dark Star who turns the enemy inward against itself with Psychological methods, trickery and technology.

Hammer family, an old mansion, no escape. They battle the nether world. Can they save the children?

Space Cadet, Clay Stone. The first Starship Captain to embark on a stellar mission to a red dwarf star

THE SAME CATALOG IN TEXT ONLY

Dark Star I   Science Fiction
Dark Star, the invisible angel of justice. The Earth is ruled by a dictatorship by a One-World Dictator gone insane.

Dark Star II   Science Fiction
This is the story of the mysterious Dark Star who turns the enemy inward against itself. Psychological methods, trickery and technology evoke justice.

Helloween   Horror
Hammer family, an old mansion, no escape. They battle the nether world. Can they save the children?

Red Dwarf   Science Fiction
Space Cadet, Clay Stone. The first Starship Captain to embark on a stellar mission to a red dwarf star

Whatever catalog design you choose, you should create an order page with instructions and pricing information.

The order page shown here is one that I prefer to use. It gives the customer several options by which they can buy the book without filling several pages of information.

To illustrate this, I have shown three different methods of connecting the buyer to the product.

1. The EBOOKS Direct button.
2. The ELECTRONIC, PAPERBACK AND HARDCOVER BOOKS menu button on the menu.
3. The individual listing of distributors and the link to each book.

The EBOOKS Direct button is the one that yields you the largest return on every sale because you net 100% of the transaction.

Unfortunately, it's the least attractive option for the customer because they have to email you, then go on to PayPal, then wait for you to email them back a book code, and then log on, enter the code and download their book.

I have it as an option because there may be a book that I don't or can't have published in the public download sites. I don't have any such nooks right now, but you never know. You might.

The ELECTRONIC, PAPERBACK AND HARDCOVER BOOKS menu button is the second list of purchasing options. This option reroutes the buyer to one (any one you choose) of the online download sites where they can purchase your books, pay and download all in one visit.

This option controls the distributor who your customer buys from. It allows you to give a distributor preferred status.

The individual listing of distributors and the link to each book is a third option that allows your buyer to choose which distributor they want to buy from. This is by far the most cumbersome of the three methods.

The individual listing of distributors can cover pages of links that confuse the buyer. If you confuse a buyer, they will often not buy.

I have included the third option with my distributor list of thirteen distributors using only four of my thirty two books. The list would suggest four times thirteen, or seventy two links for only four books.

Thirty two books would result in one hundred and twenty eight links. The list of links would be longer than the catalog contents.

OFFLINE ORDER PAGE
Choose from 7 Formats
EPUB, MOBI (Kindle), Sony, Palm, PDF, Text

INSTRUCTIONS

E = EBOOK
P = PAPERBACK
H = HARDCOVER

To direct order, send email to RobStetson@RobStetson.com indicating the name of the book you are ordering.

Then log onto PayPal and make your book payment to BobStetson@Ymail.com.

You will receive your book code for downloading the book by way of the return email.

Then, Click on the link below and enter the menu item "EBOOKS DIRECT" and download your book.

RobStetson.com   Dark Star I   E
http://www.robstetson.com/
                 Dark Star II   E
http://www.robstetson.com/
                 Helloween   E
http://www.robstetson.com/
                 Red Dwarf   E
http://www.robstetson.com/

ONLINE ORDER PAGE
Choose from 7 Formats
EPUB, MOBI (Kindle), Sony, Palm, PDF, Text

RobStetson.com   Dark Star I   E
http://www.robstetson.com/MYBOOKS3.htm
Dark Star II   E
http://www.robstetson.com/MYBOOKS3.htm
Helloween   E
http://www.robstetson.com/MYBOOKS4.htm
Red Dwarf   E
http://www.robstetson.com/MYBOOKS3.htm

Dark Star I   P
http://www.robstetson.com/MY PAPERBACKS.htm
Dark Star II   P
http://www.robstetson.com/MY PAPERBACKS.htm
Helloween   P
http://www.robstetson.com/MY PAPERBACKS.htm
Red Dwarf   P
http://www.robstetson.com/MY PAPERBACKS2.htm

Create Space   Dark Star I   P
https://createspace.com/4413607
Dark Star II   P
https://createspace.com/4469656
Helloween   P
https://createspace.com/4530028
Red Dwarf   P

https://createspace.com/4124424

Amazon   Dark Star I   E
http://www.amazon.com/Dark-Star-I-Robert-Stetson-ebook/dp/B00EU4JVEI/ref=sr_1_1?s=digital-text&ie=UTF8&qid=1386911833&sr=1-1&keywords=dark+star+i

Dark Star II   E
http://www.amazon.com/Dark-Star-II-Robert-Stetson-ebook/dp/B00G96PSWE/ref=sr_1_1?s=digital-text&ie=UTF8&qid=1386911902&sr=1-1&keywords=dark+star+ii

Helloween   E
http://www.amazon.com/Helloween-Robert-Stetson-ebook/dp/B00GRNO6J0/ref=sr_1_1?s=digital-text&ie=UTF8&qid=1386911945&sr=1-1&keywords=helloween

Red Dwarf   E
http://www.amazon.com/Red-Dwarf-ebook/dp/B00AX8VNAK/ref=sr_1_1?s=digital-text&ie=UTF8&qid=1378934613&sr=1-1&keywords=red+dwarf

Lulu   Dark Star I   E
http://www.lulu.com/shop/robert-stetson/dark-star-i/ebook/product-21216632.html

Dark Star II   E
http://www.lulu.com/shop/robert-stetson/dark-star-ii/ebook/product-21237159.html

Helloween   E
http://www.lulu.com/shop/robert-stetson/helloween/ebook/product-21259194.html

Red Dwarf　　E
http://www.lulu.com/shop/robert-stetson/red-dwarf/ebook/product-21015434.html

Smashwords　　　　　Dark Star I　　E
https://www.smashwords.com/books/view/350067
Dark Star II　E
https://www.smashwords.com/books/view/364287
Helloween　　E
https://www.smashwords.com/books/view/368600
Red Dwarf　　E
https://www.smashwords.com/books/view/271910

Barnes and Noble   Dark Star I   E
http://www.barnesandnoble.com/w/dark-star-i-robert-stetson/1116664980?ean=9781492231523
Dark Star II   E
http://www.barnesandnoble.com/w/dark-star-ii-robert-stetson/1117080043?ean=9781304510945
Helloween   E
http://www.barnesandnoble.com/w/helloween-robert-stetson/1117184100?ean=9781493796779
Red Dwarf   E
http://www.barnesandnoble.com/w/red-dwarf-robert-stetson/1114232604?ean=2940015944518&itm=1&usri=2940015944518

Barnes and Noble   Dark Star I   P
http://www.barnesandnoble.com/w/dark-star-i-robert-stetson/1116664980?ean=9781492231523
Dark Star II   P
http://www.barnesandnoble.com/w/dark-star-i-robert-stetson/1116664980?ean=9781492231523
Helloween   P
http://www.barnesandnoble.com/w/helloween-robert-stetson/1117184100?ean=9781493796779
Red Dwarf   P
http://www.barnesandnoble.com/w/red-dwarf-robert-stetson/1114232604?ean=9781481934220

Xinxii Dark Star I   Dark Star I   E

http://www.xinxii.com/en/dark-star-p-346197.html
Dark Star II   E
http://www.xinxii.com/en/dark-star-ii-p-347186.html
Helloween   E
http://www.xinxii.com/en/helloween-p-347567.html
Red Dwarf   E
http://www.xinxii.com/en/red-dwarf-p-340859.html

Book Country   Dark Star I   E
http://bookstore.bookcountry.com/Products/SKU-000684739/Dark-Star-I.aspx
                      Dark Star II   E
http://bookstore.bookcountry.com/Products/SKU-000694951/Dark-Star-II.aspx
                      Helloween   E
http://bookstore.bookcountry.com/Products/SKU-000702583/Helloween.aspx
                      Red Dwarf   E
http://bookstore.bookcountry.com/Products/SKU-000681180/Red-Dwarf.aspx

Feed a Read   Red Dwarf   E
http://www.feedaread.com/books/Red-Dwarf-9781782998464.aspx

WaveCloud   Dark Star I   E
https://www.wavecloud.com/book/dark-star-i/wc20000111561/11888446
                      Dark Star II   E
https://www.wavecloud.com/book/dark-star-ii/wc20000111666/12219866
                      Helloween   E
https://www.wavecloud.com/book/helloween/wc20000111690/12246831
                      Red Dwarf   E

https://www.wavecloud.com/book/red-dwarf/wc20000111434/11433441

Kobo   Dark Star I   E
http://store.kobobooks.com/en-US/ebook/dark-star-i-1
                     Dark Star II   E
http://store.kobobooks.com/en-US/ebook/dark-star-ii-2
                     Helloween   E
http://store.kobobooks.com/en-US/ebook/helloween-1
                     Red Dwarf   E
http://store.kobobooks.com/en-US/ebook/red-dwarf-1

Google Dark Star I E
https://play.google.com/store/books/details?id=LTmuAAAAQBAJ
Dark Star II E
https://play.google.com/store/books/details?id=PaAcAgAAQBAJ
Helloween E
https://play.google.com/store/books/details/Robert_Stetson_Helloween?id=Q6IcAgAAQBAJ
Red Dwarf E
https://play.google.com/store/books/details/Robert_Stetson_Red_Dwarf?id=QYKSAAAAQBAJ
All Romance Red Dwarf E
https://www.allromanceebooks.com/product-reddwarf-1209597-153.html

Flea markets are not always cheap and they will run anywhere from $ 35 and up for a table for the day.

Still, it gives you the opportunity to make hundreds of contacts, but I recommend you have a lot of books on a variety of topics and some way for people to log on and get their books.

The download option for your website is always a good way to get them their books from home later.

Use the instructions on how to make your website a secure download place.

I recommend you have 10 coded copies of each book and have the tickets preprinted with the unique book identifiers and ready to sell.

The beauty of this method is that they don't have to email you, use PayPal or wait for you to email them back with a password. They just give you the money and you give them the ticket with the password for their particular book right there on the spot.

You can also have a couple of copies of your books right there in Paperback to sell.

There are bookstores out there that will let you set up a card table and present your work for free.

Some Book Stores will allow it, while others won't. Speak to the store manager about their policies.

The downside to having a book signing is that the public has to buy your book, and then you have to sign it.

To accomplish that, you have to buy a few, or several, of your printed books on speculation.

If no one buys your book, you will be the proud owner of several copies.

You can wallpaper your place with the pages, or give them away as gifts. I don't recommend this strategy for selling books unless you are super confident.

Another strategy for retailing your books in a neighborhood bookstore is to talk the manager into putting your books on the shelf for sale and on consignment.

There is a retail attitude that says, "Shelf space has value", so you're taking up space the store is theoretically paying rent for.

Be prepared to be told to pick up your books if they don't sell within a reasonable time frame. If they don't sell, your back in the same boat you were in before you did the book signing.

The advantage of consignment is that you can just put one or two on the shelf. That's not a lot to be stuck with.

What would be a reasonable consignment percentage? That's negotiable.

There are two kinds of bulletin boards. You have the electronic bulletin boards featured on cable TV and web sites, and there are the bulletin boards you see around town in big supermarkets and other local business establishments

Attaching business cards to a bulletin board is a little tricky. I find that using thumb tacks stuck through two or three cards is somewhat (forgive the pun) tacky.

I have included the plans for making your own business card holders that attach to the bulletin board with two thumb tacks. The advantage to the business card holder is that people don't tend to steal the thumb tacks from them, and the business cards don't start looking like someone took a shotgun to them.

Another advantage of the holder is that it looks more professional and you can put ten or twelve cards in them at a time without difficulty.

The plans allow you to use post card stock or thicker, to easily create them in volume.

Although the card holder shown here will hold at least a couple dozen cards, I limit the number of cards to ten or twelve.

It makes it easier for someone to remove a card without spilling the rest. It creates the impression that others are taking them.

For some reason, when millions of people have purchased a product, you're supposed to want one too.

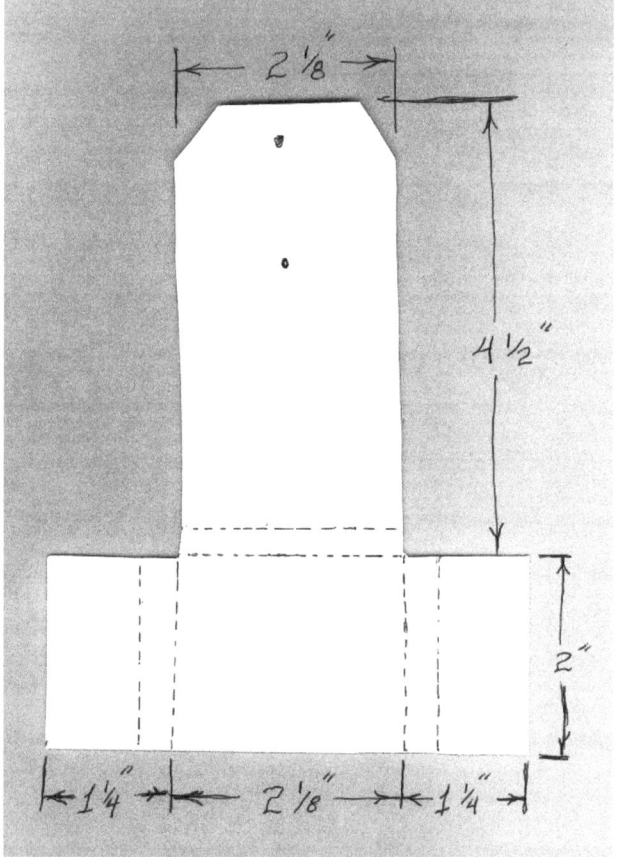

The diagram above is a photocopy of a card holder showing the overall dimensions.

Make sure you use a heavy enough stock so it doesn't tear or come apart on the bulletin board.

In all the years I have used these, it has never been necessary for me to replace the card holder.

I'm not sure why, but people steal each other's tacks and trash their flyers, but not these.

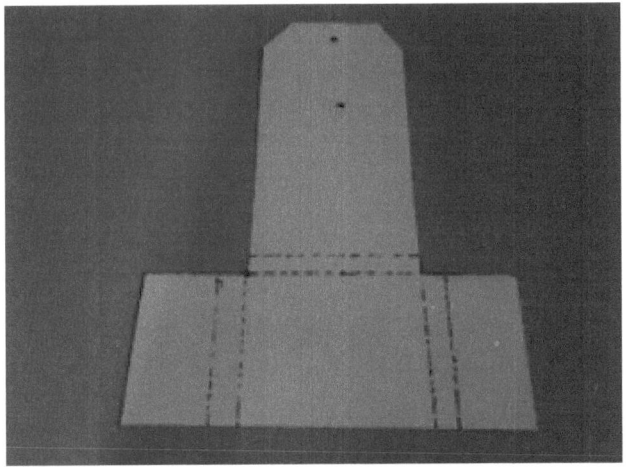

Cut the holder from the card stock as shown here. The dotted lines indicate where the folds will go.

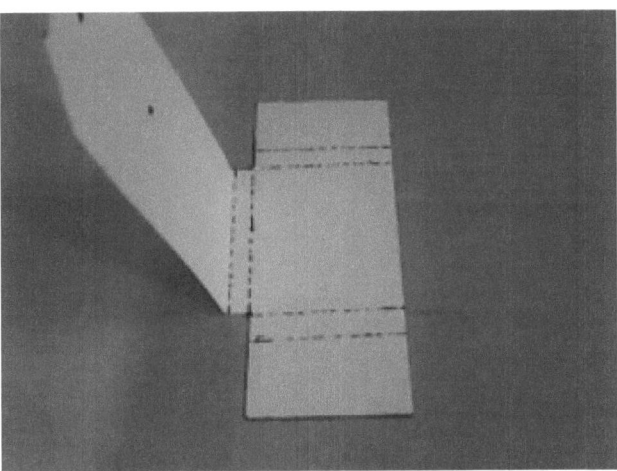

Fold the back up as shown here to form the part that will be thumbtacked to the bulletin board.

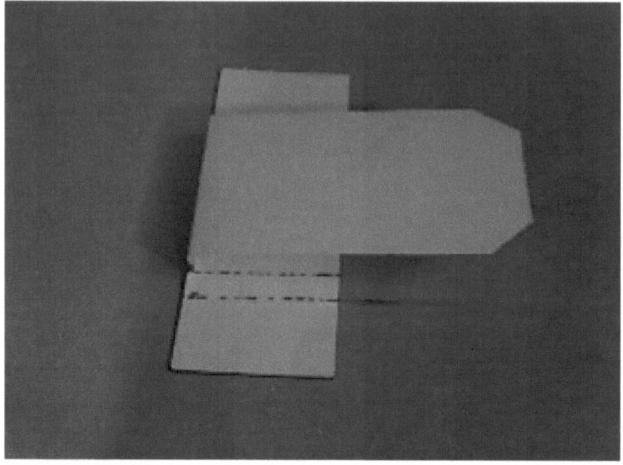

Fold the back up again to form a "U".

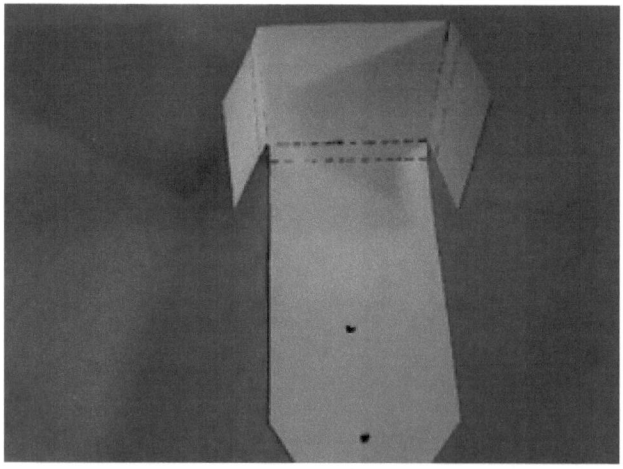

Now you can bend the bottom part and the side flaps to bring the front of the holder around so that it's ready to wrap around the holder and form a flat cup to hold the business cards.

Now that you have the flaps ready to attach to the back of the holder, you notice the whole thing is a bit flimsy.

To stiffen things up a bit so you can work on it, just stack it chuck full of business cards so you can firmly tape the back flaps to the unit and have a sturdy flat cup in the front.

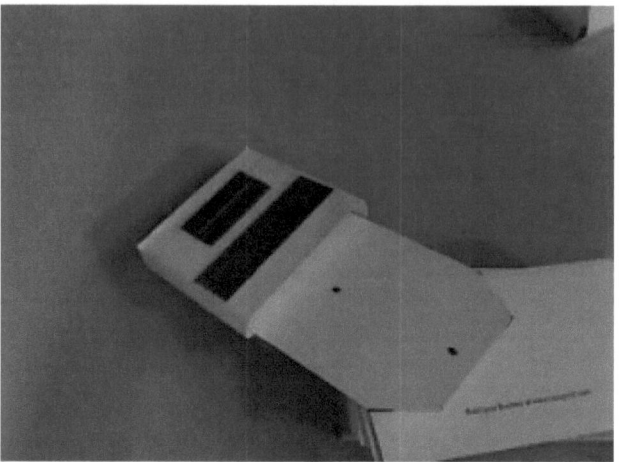

Here is a view of the completed card holder ready to thumbtack to a bulletin board.

The back is firmly taped on with plain old scotch tape. If you use good solid card stock to make the business card holder, it will be amazing just how sturdy it will be.

Let the artist inside of you run free. You can cut selected areas from your cards and attach them to the front of the holder.

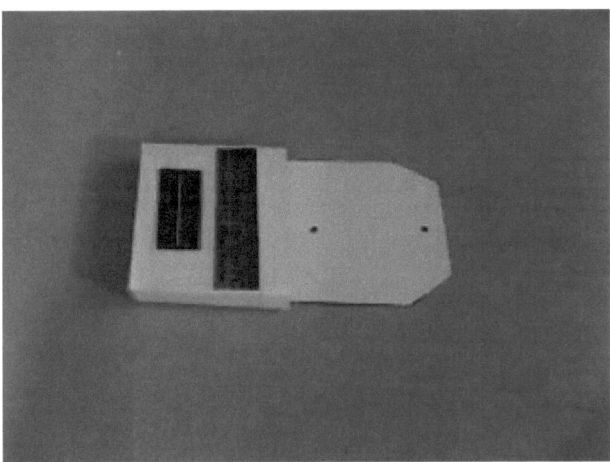

Notice the two dots I have put in the top portion of the holder? These are where the flat headed thumbtacks go.

Don't use those plastic thumb tacks with the protruding grips to aid you in removing the tack.

Having the flat thumbtacks will not only make it easier to remove cards and refill the holder when it's empty, but it will make it harder for those thumbtack-thieves to remove your tacks so they can put something else up there.

I use two thumb tacks to prevent the holder from rotating and spilling your cards on the floor (no one ever seems to pick them up and put them back).

You can buy plastic or wooden business card holders, but don't do that. A dollar here and a dollar there, pretty soon you have spent two dollars.

If you think I'm just being cheap, consider the situation that evolves from investing in your bulletin board advertising.

You pay a dollar for an attractive business card holder and place it at the Mall. Next week you stop by to see if you need to replace any missing cards and the holder is gone.

The cards might have been stuck aside, or they may have just been thrown away, but someone has absconded with your business card holder.

CHAPTER 10 MANAGE PRICING

This would be the normal way of establishing the product pricing schedule. Not all stores are going to want to get involved in the eBook pricing strategy. Some may expect you to run it as a business from your end.

Whether you have a firm strategy that requires the store to establish pricing, or whether you have a firm requirement that the store accepts your pricing strategy, the policy could cost you distribution channels. I recommend you go with the distributor's preference at this point.

If the distributor defers pricing to you, that would mean pricing guidelines put in place by you. Pricing guidelines are just that, guidelines. They are not policies or rules.

For paperbacks and hardcover books, be sure and use the cost plus shipping and handling to obtain the books and then add on a reasonable profit. Make sure there is enough margin for both you and the store owner.

The pricing structure for eBooks has to be competitive with the online distributors, but the good news is that you don't have to buy the books, you already own them in software form.

The terms of service for most online distributors states that you can't charge less than their price elsewhere. This is true for eBooks only.

The online distributors want you to compete fairly and not undercut them on sales pricing.

I generally just take the online distributor's retail price and apply it to offline sales. Some online distributors will discount your books. If they do, you can match their retail discounted price as long as you're not selling the books cheaper than they are.

Bear in mind that every time you discount a book, you cut into the profits for both you and your storefront distributors.

CHAPTER 11 MARKETING YOUR WARES

Just as with pricing, the question of advertising could be a sticky wicket. Let the distributor do as they wish with regard to advertising.

Unlike selling, which is the linking of customers to your products for the exchange of money, marketing is making people aware of your products. Advertising is marketing. Book signings and your distributors are sales (selling). There is a difference.

This is where I recommend that you take the most economical routes possible. Your net profits are going to be small, as a rule, and advertising is an expensive proposition.

There are hundreds of free or nearly free opportunities out there if you know how to tap into them. VistaPrint is one of them.

You can get 250 free business cards and all you do is pay the postage. For less than $4 more, they sent me 500 cards. That's still under $10 for 500 cards at 2 cents apiece. Shop around and you will quickly realize just how good a deal that is.

Apply the target market concept by not just ordering cards for every book you publish without knowing one of two things.

Having a niche market identified is knowing where the people are who would like your book. A book for or about commuters would benefit from the business cards in a bus or train station, or maybe an airport.

One of the first things you want to do is give your book its own business card. Sound strange? Well, you will get used to the idea as soon as you realize that your book can take on a life of its own.

Like a child who has grown and is ready to enter the world on their own, we tend to cling to them, never regarding them as able to fend for themselves. Be a good parent. Let go of the book and set it free. If it can stand on its own it will come back to visit in the form of royalties.

You can always lend a helping hand to foster your book career, like promotions, advertising, uploading to new markets or book signings. Like a child of whom you are proud, you also have to let go and foster the growth of other books in order to make your list of publications grow.

Today's EBook market is getting harder and harder to make money at because everyone's getting into the act and it might seem like fewer people are reading.

The truth is that writers are doing just the opposite of what they ought to be doing.

When times are really tough for the oil companies, they raise their prices. Sorry... Bad example...

They raise their prices to offset lost profits, but then, when times are good the increased demand signals them to raise prices as well.

Our problem is that when the sales are off because more and more people are taking free books, writers drop their price in the hopes of making a sale.

When the prices fall, writers drop them even more to get to the bottom of the average asking price.

We're killing each other!

Set a fair price and insist on it. Raise awareness of your book and hold firm on a fair asking price. I make sales without giving my books away.

This book is your answer to lower prices. You are making little enough without spending a lot of money on advertising. That's why we're here.

You can certainly have a bundle of traditional business cards made for you if you like. I'm advocating a whole different kind of business card.

How many times have you been given a business card with a picture of a book cover, what it's about, the price and where to buy it?

The cards are the kind you leave around town for 2 cents each

So, what goes on my cards? Let's make a couple and see how it goes.

For openers, I want to show you the first Book Business card I ever made.

It doesn't look as bad when you scan it, but there is a problem with it.

It's too dark, which makes it too hard to read.

I'm sharing my mistakes with you so you don't make them too. I have to open my kimono (in a manner of speaking) and not be too proud or this book won't work nearly as well for you.

If all I share are my successes, you might wonder why they aren't working for you. That would be because you risk mixing success with failure every time you start to grow in a new direction.

Now that we know what to avoid when building a book-business-card, let's take a look at how to make a more effective card.

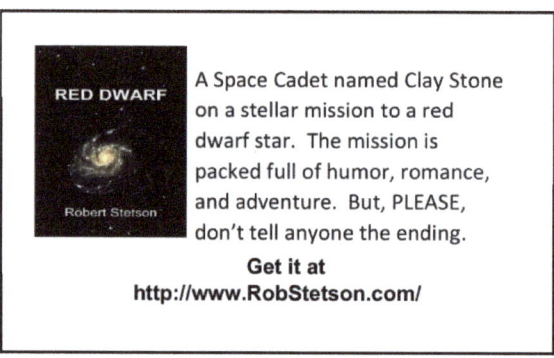

Nothing sells a book like a spiffy cover and a good synopsis. You can see the cover image looks good, but the description is a bit too brief. There isn't room for a great synopsis. You just have to do the best you can with the space you have.

Never put the price on the card unless it will compel someone to buy. At $3.99 for an EBook download, the fair price is not compelling, so I left it off.

The URL address isn't for one of my book distributors. I use my website to allow the user to choose the format, EBook, Paperback, Hardcover, etc. If the user chooses the EBook format (it costs a lot less), then they can choose between several formats depending on the type of reader they own.

As an incentive to buy my books I also offer a FREE EBook Reader for the P.C. that can be downloaded and installed. When there is room on the card without overcrowding I mention the FREE Reader.

Experience has taught me to favor a white card because colors make the message less easy to read.

If you're looking for the maximum contrast, it's not black on white as you might imagine, but is black on yellow.

The cards are free because VistaPrint put their web address on the back of the card. I'm impressed with how unobtrusive it is and that it's so small.

The beauty of these little advertising nuggets is in the fact that you can carry them in your pocket. They're always there when you see a chance to plant the seed.

Always look at the ROI (Return On Investment) when considering a marketing strategy.

Let's imagine you get a 3% sales return on 100 cards. Let's also imagine you make $3.49 royalty. Your royalty on 3 sales is $10.47.

At 2 cents each, 100 VistaPrint business card sized flyers would cost $2. Your net return on the investment is $8.47. That's $8.47 more than you would have had if you hadn't spent the $2.

Let's consider a radio advertisement if you were to get the spot for $300 for a whole month. You would have to sell 86 books just to break even.

Most people who hear a radio ad are driving and have their hands full of steering wheel.

Even if they like the sound of the book, they don't have a pencil. The next car that cuts them off or obscene gesture will erase the memory of your book.

Besides, remember what I told you about in your face (in your ear) unsolicited advertising.

Do you eat out? Do you leave a tip? One good turn deserves another. Leave a business card flyer (or 2) on the table with the tip. If you charmed the waitperson during dinner, they may read your 2 cent card and consider your book.

You can drop (oops!) a card on just about any counter or washroom sink area.

Always remember to heed the BIG TABOOS at the end of this book.

If you anger the book retailers remember that your EBook is circulated to them in the online books and catalogs.

People in the book retail industry will talk amongst themselves. You will be blackballed. Never compete with your own sales channels. Win, lose or draw, you lose.

I'm rather proud of my book covers because the artwork is excellent. I seldom create my own artwork with the exception of this book.

For this book I spread out fifteen $100 bills on my scanner and made the background for the book. The cover came out fine and I got to keep the money.

Ninety nine percent of the time I get my artwork online at http://www.public-domain-image.com/.

There are several sites that offer free public domain images. Be very careful when you download images to make sure they are public domain. An angry photographer can make your life miserable and get your book removed from the market.

Once in a while there just doesn't seem to be anything out there that quite does the trick.

I was looking for demon eyes and there are plenty out there, but I wasn't 100% sure that the ones I liked were public domain. Unless it says "Public Domain" don't take any chances.

Don't trust every site to be truly public domain. Only use sites you trust and that you can go back to if there is a question to show that you had every right to believe they are public domain. It pays to be paranoid.

Pay attention to the type style. Make sure it's readable. Some types are hard to read because they're too fancy or specialized, such as some fonts used at Halloween.

Remember to keep it simple, concise and clear. The image should be striking in some respect and convey the flavor of the book.

Sometimes I take a public domain image and stretch it, crop it, or flip it over to get the effect I want like this one.

A compelling photo will catch the eye

It's just odd enough to draw someone's attention to the card, or the book cover.

Anything you want in high volume can be done at VistaPrint and the shipping is cheap.

After paying the cost of shipping and having the business card sized brochures increased from 250 free cards to 500 cards for less than $10.00, I think the whole deal was fantastic.

They also do tri-fold brochures, invitations and a host of other products.

On the subject of flyers, don't overcrowd your flyer. The message is simple, "Buy my book," right?

The basic ad flyer has three elements. It identifies you. It identifies your product; it tells where the product can be obtained.

Unlike utilitarian products that are described with their features and benefits, the flyer is selling a more aesthetic product.

Either way, the object is to make the reader want to purchase it.

To accomplish this we have to go back to basics and remember that people don't read they scan. For someone to pick up your flyer and look at it, something has to catch their eye. That thing to catch their eye would be the cover image.

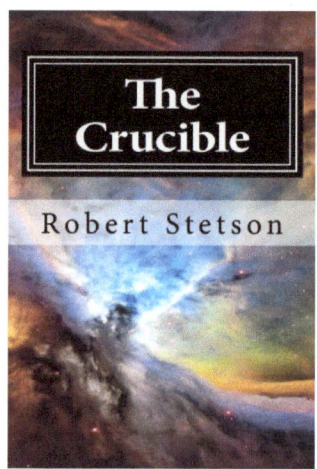

A compelling cover will naturally peak their curiosity causing them to take a closer look at the description.

The second most important part of the flyer is the description. If the description doesn't capture their interest, they will move on.

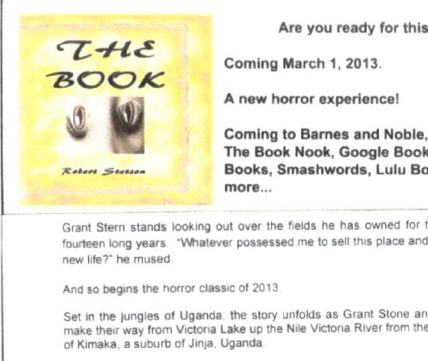

Flyers are one of the cheapest forms of advertising for your books. Aside from the cost of ink or toner and the cost of a sheet of paper, the advertising medium is free.

The real trick here is how to get the flyers into the hands of willing readers without aggravating anyone. I wish I could say that's simple, but it needs to be addressed with care. It can be done if you look at the problem from the reader's point of view.

Consider your own reaction to advertising.

If someone thrusts a flyer in your face while you're walking down the street, your first reaction is to throw it away. The act was an intrusion.

If you log into your Email and find six pieces of SPAM in your Email, you delete them without a glance.

If you find a flyer stuck under your windshield wiper blade, you throw it away and think, "How dare they touch my car?"

When the phone rings and it's a robot voice saying, "Please remain on the line for an important message." You hang up in disgust at the intrusion on your privacy.

Get the idea?

What if you're leaving a shop, or entering a phone booth (Are there any left?) and see a business card or flyer about a book. You might look at it if the image is interesting. The difference is that you decided to voluntarily consider the ad worth the time.

The message here is to always let the reader discover your ad.

The second message is that, in general, once a person makes a buying decision, they tend to defend the decision to buy.

So once you get a reader hooked on the idea of buying your book, they will generally regard their decision as a wise one.

A perfect example of this is a car or motorcycle purchase. The vehicle has to be pretty bad for the buyer to regret their decision. New car buyers tend to strut around like bantam roosters and display pride in their new vehicle.

People who buy a book (actually pay for it) are less critical than people who download a free EBook.

That's simply because of the phenomenon known as "Perceived Value".

If you want bad reviews, just put your book out there for free. Almost as bad is the tactic of pricing a full length novel at 99 cents.

Some of my works have been priced at as little as $1.99 because they were 39 pages or less and were an easy read. An underpriced book will not sell well.

Getting back to the topic of flyers never put the price on your flyer. You would be asking the buyer to make a value judgment without looking into the content.

Flyers can cost more than the VistaPrint mini business card brochures discussed in the last chapter. The kicker is in the cost of ink. The ink jet printer is the most expensive method of printing because of the ridiculous cost of ink cartridges.

That brings us to the question of whether or not to make your flyers full color or black and white.

I guess that depends on what you mean by full color. Remember the flyer we made earlier?

Are you ready for this?

Coming March 1, 2013.

A new horror experience!

Coming to Barnes and Noble, Amazon The Book Nook, Google Books, Hugo Books, Smashwords, Lulu Books, and more...

Grant Stern stands looking out over the fields he has owned for the last fourteen long years. "Whatever possessed me to sell this place and start a new life?" he mused.

And so begins the horror classic of 2013.

Set in the jungles of Uganda, the story unfolds as Grant Stone and Molly make their way from Victoria Lake up the Nile Victoria River from the village of Kimaka, a suburb of Jinja, Uganda.

The evil book of glyphs is unearthed at an Archeological Dig. The locals recognize it as "The Book of Demons".

Does the Devil have a Bible?
Can the world stand against the power unleashed?

Cry, weep, scream, but please, don't give away the ending.

Get this and 14 other Horror, Sci-Fi, and Training Manuals by Robert Stetson at;

http://www.RobStetson.com/

Notice that there is a splash of color, but to keep the printing cost down to a manageable level, I didn't make it look like a circus poster.

You're not advertising a circus where the barkers and game booths are going to rake in thousands of dollars per day. You're not marketing a movie with a poster that will yield millions in revenue.

You have to assume your humble book sales will possibly average $500 per year, more or less, per book depending on your non-exclusive contract and the royally deal.

The websites offering 100% royalty to you will have a much lower sales volume than the Internet monsters like Amazon with a 35% royalty.

If you're wondering why I'm so obsessed with the book prices, royalties, projected volume sales and all the rest, then you haven't picked up on the idea that this book isn't about selling a lot of books.

It's about making more money on the sale of books than you spend on marketing.

Our marketing game is very different from the general marketing business. If you over-market your book, you will lose money even though you sell ten times more books.

A smart marketer will always be crunching the numbers on the cost. Figure out what you pay for a ream (500 sheets) of paper. Then take the average number of sheets per ink cartridge or toner cartridge.

Calculate the cost of printing 500 sheets of paper based on the average cost per sheet you got from the statistics.

Add the cost of ink or toner for 500 sheets against the cost for a ream of paper and then divide by 500.

Now you have the cost of printing a single brochure. Don't forget to add in the cost of color ink or toner.

Multiply that by 100 and take three percent of that number times the royalty for each book and you have the projected rate of return for a campaign using 100 flyers.

If your response to the flyers is 3% you're doing fine. Those were the statistics when the market was healthy. If you get 1% don't be disappointed.

Don't drive all over town planting your ads. The cost of gasoline is a killer. Flyers and brochures are just an opportunity based advertising campaign.

Most people tend to forget. Your time has value too. Keep the time you spend on advertising to a reasonable level.

If you're out spreading flyers, you're not writing. Don't lose sight of the reason your publishing. People will find and buy your books anyway. We're just trying to grease the skids on our sales numbers.

Unlike business correspondence, the paper used for your flyers doesn't matter. Use the cheapest possible paper, such as copy machine paper that you buy on sale by the case (10 reams).

You can also get ink jet and toner refills online at half the cost at your local retail store businesses.

If you're shopping for bargains online be sure and keep a spare ink jet cartridge and/or toner cartridge on hand.

Don't get caught short. It takes a week or two to get a cartridge in the mail.

If you keep a backup, you can pay the lowest price for shipping and the week or two won't put you out of business.

Does shopping online make you nervous? It should. There are a lot of hucksters out there. I do my online ink and toner business with Ink Plus Toner. http://www.inkplustoner.com/

When you order ink or toner cartridges, don't forget to add in the cost of shipping when comparing their prices to the local merchants.

If you get it for 80% of the coast and then pay shipping, do you really save money? You need to sharpen your pencil and figure out just how much the product is costing.

Tax considerations need to be taken into consideration also. There is sales tax on your supplies and there is the withholding tax on your royalties. Good business practice dictates that you account for the sales tax as part of the basic cost of goods. Your local retailer will always charge for sales tax, while many online sellers will not charge sales tax.

Make Shure you keep a ledger of all your expenses along with taxes to include sales tax because all of this is tax deductible.

It's bad enough to have your royalties dwindles down to pennies after expenses without having to pay tax on the gross income.

A free preview flyer would contain a few paragraphs from your book to give the reader a nibble. The sample should be compelling enough to make anyone want to read more. It should be the hopefully interesting table of contents.

The text that follows shouldn't be more than the first chapter or so taken from the book. No one is going to read much more.

If the first chapter grabs their interest, they will want to buy the book; otherwise the preview will go in the trash.

We're looking at about a dozen or so pages which makes this form of flyer a bit expensive to make. I would put a nice, but inexpensive cover on it to add to the appeal.

A nice cover will make the whole thing look more professional and people will be more likely to pick it up and look inside.

If your product is erotica, don't even bother making a preview flyer. It would be deemed unsuitable for children and no one wants erotica displayed in their shop.

Any shop that would allow erotica to be displayed would be your competitor. They would most likely be selling erotica too. This falls under the BIG TABOO list at the end of the book.

Given the high cost of this new marketing strategy, you will have to apply some special rules.

Any book you do this for will need to be a good seller. If the book is sold in good volume, then this will work in carefully planned locations.

If you have a book with a narrow target audience, the only way you can turn it to your advantage would be to know where you want to drop the flyers.

If your book is about boating then a yacht club is a perfect place, but make sure they will allow you to put them there before you make a dozen or so.

Be careful with target marketing. It's tricky. For instance a book of do-it-yourself Pizza Recipes would be a bombshell if left in a pizzeria, sub-shop or a restaurant. The best place for such a book would be a mini-mart or grocery store where people could buy the ingredients.

With a little creative thinking and a few carefully invested dollars you can do magic.

There's nothing new about the concept of the preview flyer.

When you log on to Amazon or other web sites, you can click on the cover of the book cover illustration and read the first ten or twenty percent of the book. This is the same idea, but they don't have to log on anywhere to see the preview.

One thing about impulse viewing of flyers is that if you don't grab their interest in the first paragraph, they will move on.

Unlike the book preview on the book seller's web site, the reader wasn't shopping for a book when they started reading.

It goes without saying that the compelling photo will peak the curiosity of a passerby. It's the best you can hope for.

In the event that your cover photo isn't as compelling as you might like, who says you are confined to that image?

Select an image that's a grabber, then a description that compels the reader to look further. You have converted a disinterested passerby into a prospective customer.

It's all done by getting one sale here, and one sale there. One by one, you start having sales that you wouldn't have ordinarily made. After a while, these numbers add up.

There are things you should never, ever do. These things will gain you enemies, turn new friends against you, or become legal hassles.

Taboo # 1; never put your adverting literature anywhere on the property of a bookstore or a place that sells books. That goes for their parking lot or outside of their building.

Taboo # 2, you must never make a new friend, and then start talking about them buying your books.

Taboo # 3, you must never hand out your literature in person to anyone you don't know without a good reason.

Taboo # 4, you must never put your literature in any store unless you ask for permission first.

Taboo # 5, you must never send unsolicited Email to anyone who knows you in order to sell your books.

Taboo # 6, you must never SPAM.

Taboo # 7, Avoid binding "agreements" or binding "contracts". They never favor you.

Taboo # 8, never cover or obscure the Vista Print URL on the back of the free card. It was given to you for free at Vista Print's expense. It would be discourteous to defeat their ad.

Taboo # 9, do not attempt to advertise erotica to the general public or in a XXX bookstore. Erotica is a private thing and should be confined to the distribution channels. Let the resellers market your product. They have the distribution channels, you don't.

Taboo # 10, don't get involved with the retail end of the business. It's a full time job and some people will absorb all of your time with questions and problems.

Write, and leave the business end to the retail business people. That's what your sales are paying them to do.

Sell your EBooks and printed books with a cut for the store. Issue one time passwords to confirm and enable downloads.

I've already shown you how to create the tickets for each book. Make sure you give the store owner tickets for each of the books you want to sell, but keep the number of each book ticket low. Perhaps two or three each.

These tickets are like cash, so print the value on each of them. If you want to cash in, the missing tickets are sales. If the store manager loses a ticket, that's a sale.

Books would be downloaded from your website in text or PDF readable on any computer.

Now I'll tell you how to source all the converted files for your website for free.

This is the wonderful part of having files converted for you.

For example, on Smashwords, you can upload a standard format with non-smashword copyright notice, standard "Heading 1" headers and all. You will get "Vetter" errors, but that's OK. Go to "My Smashwords", then double click on the book title you want and you go to the sales page.

Click on the link "You own it, Download. It will take you to a download page where you can get the file in every format you converted it to when you published it.

Upload the book in a properly formatted Smashwords format when you're done.

Now you have the converted files ready for the other sites and you have a properly formatted book on Smashwords ready for sale.

As far as marketing and advertising goes, take this warning very seriously. There is a blizzard of "FREE" ad opportunities that are not free! The latest scam is to get you there, be vague about the terms and then you discover that they meant "Try it for FREE", which means sign up for free and we will bill you later.

Some free offers are constructed in such a way that you enter a free deal, but to make it work at all you really have to add on some not so free extras along the way.

You find more and more FREE stuff out there, such offers as, "Free for 30 days", or "Try it for free", or "Free, just pay postage and handling", and I could go on and on.

My biggest gripe is when a company says, "Sign up for our low cost deal. Only $ 19 a month". Now you're supposed to be thinking, "Wow, I'm paying $ 39 a month. I could be paying only $ 19 a month".

The fine print tells you it's for the first three months, but they never tell you how much it will be three months after you commit to their product.

Doesn't it strike you as odd how they never tell you how much it will be when the "first three months" are up? Now you're signed up with a contract, a termination penalty and a monthly bill of $ 59 a month.

I don't generally get involved with online fee related sites simply because there are fees involved in selling there. Each little nibble at your wallet subtracts from your sales.

You can easily pay more than you generate in revenues when you set yourself up on a site where you are charged on a monthly basis for services along with possible posting and transaction fees.

It doesn't make sense to end up with $ .35 out of every dollar, or worse, maybe paying $ 1.22 for every dollar in sales after the posting; monthly management and commissions are tallied up.

In all fairness to E-Advertisers, I haven't really looked at the fee schedules there, but there are fee schedules and that goes against my marketing policies. If you venture there, make sure you are aware of the cost.

Why get sucked into a contract that you can't get out of when there is so much offered for free?

Places like http://www.CraigsList.com are free and you can post there, but have a website where people can connect and buy without involving you directly in the transaction, unless you don't mind being busy doing retail sales.

CHAPTER 12 DEALING WITH PIRACY

BEFORE WE BEGIN..

I am not an Attorney, nor do I pretend to interpret the law or seek to represent anyone. My advice here is procedural with regard to how to file a complaint and where to file it. As for legal advice, seek an Attorney if you are concerned about the legalities.

When it comes to procedural issues beyond filing a complaint, I recommend you seek legal advice.

As a past Licensed Private Detective, working Internet issues out of my offices in two states, I offer my past experience.

There are a couple of things you should consider. First, a pirate will misspell your name and/or the name of your book in the listings. Just because you don't see your book listed anywhere, it doesn't mean someone out there on the Internet isn't either giving it away or selling it.

They know you will be looking for your books. They really don't care if the book is listed properly. A book is a book. When someone downloads the book, the name and title will be correct. They don't actually edit the book.

Overall I find that from an international perspective, you can't judge the responsiveness of Internet Service Providers based on the American response to piracy.

If you think the Internet websites don't take it seriously, just let someone accuse you of piracy or plagiarism. Your books will be removed.

Oddly enough, piracy is (I have read) a civil matter in the United States, but accusing someone of piracy and falsifying the report is a criminal act (perjury). Go figure. Other countries have their own legal systems and are not governed by United States Law.

The saving grace is that there are international sites where the laws are apparently tougher. The United States has joined these groups and these groups are much more active with regard to piracy.

One such group is the DMCA, or "Digital Millennium Copyright Act" They have a "Digital Millennium Copyright Act Takedown Notice" that is policed by the DMCA

The DMCA can enforce the rules regarding copyrighted materials when the proper procedures are followed.

The ICANN, or Internet Corporation for Assigned Names and Numbers has strict rules regarding the operation of websites. Copyright violations and viruses are not tolerated.

If you file a complaint with them, they do take it seriously and will investigate the matter. ICANN is located in California, USA.

I should warn you that while law enforcement in most countries take eBook piracy seriously, I have read that the Supreme Court of the United States does not regard eBook piracy as a crime. They have

(I understand) classified piracy of eBooks as a civil matter.

It leads me to wonder if the stern warnings on the front end of movies are a scare tactic, or whether the Supreme Court has no respect for the intellectual property rights of independent authors.

I digress.

DEALING WITH PIRACY

The first rule in dealing with piracy is, don't. Don't deal with them. You have to stop it in its tracks. Trying to reason with them is like trying to reason with a subway robber. If they had a shred of honor, they wouldn't be thieves.

As one person put it, giving them your credit card info, or signing on as a web customer in order to find your books would be like throwing your money clip into a dark alley to see if there are any thieves in there.

Let's imagine your books have been stolen. At first you might feel powerless. This is true especially because they won't remove your copyrighted material. You have far more power than you realize.

Since time is money, you want to resolve this as soon as possible. Follow a clear and deliberate path. Don't be in such a hurry that you start filing complaints without gathering information.

Go to Google and in the search window type the name of the book. I have used my book, "*HOW DISK DRIVES WORK*" as an example.

Type in (I used NO suffix.) I entered HOW DISK DRIVES WORK in the search field. You will be swamped with items. My book didn't even get listed on the first couple of pages. So enter "HOW DISK DRIVES WORK Robert Stetson". I have added the author's name after the book title.

Now you get the pages all about me and *HOW DISK DRIVES WORK* written by me. You can put

.Epub, but the info will be filtered and your results will not be as robust.

Using no filename extension will allow you to see if the file was converted to another format.

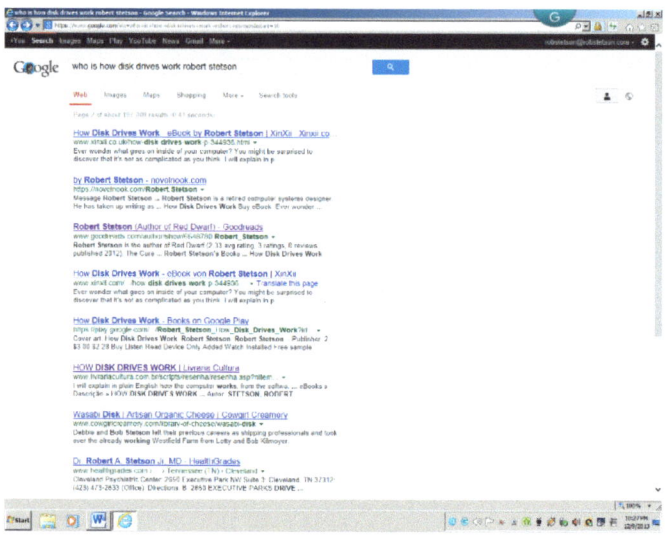

You can see that my book was published and put up for download on several websites. As I scan down the page, I see a listing for HOW DISK DRIVES WORK being offered by Livraria Cultura and I'm not familiar with that Brazilian website, so I click on the link to look at my book listing and it's all there.

They are not giving the book away for free. It's priced at R6.67. The numerical denomination is called the Rand and the exchange rate causes the price to be listed at "R6.67" even though the book is listed at "$3.99" in American currency.

Now I have to wonder, are they pirating my book and selling it on the open market?

DIRECT SELL YOUR EBOOKS OFFLINE

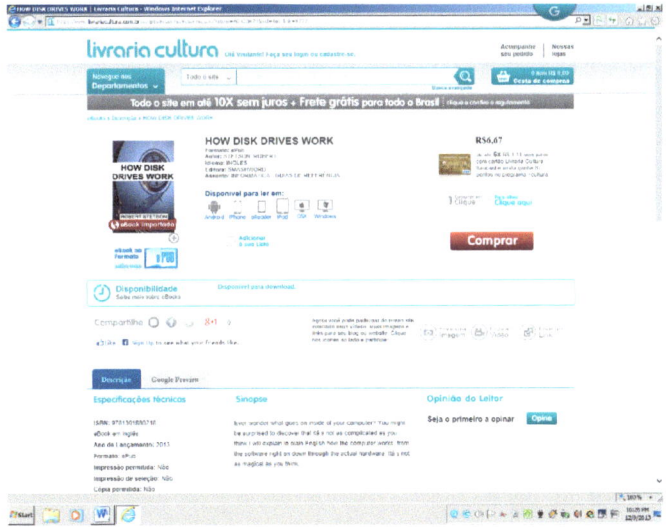

Be very careful when scouting around for pirate copies of your books. Livraria Cultura turns out to be a legitimate distributor that is outsourced from Smashwords where I have my book listed.

When Livraria Cultura sells a copy of my book, the royalty comes back to me as a sale through Smashwords.

I have fourteen primary distributors where I signed up and uploaded my books for sale. Those fourteen distributors each has several sub-distributors, some of which I never heard of, as you can see.

If I were to start a Takedown notice against this website, I would be creating a nightmare for myself. They are legal and I would be cutting my own financial throat.

I also have to wonder what Smashwords would have to say about me bullying one of their sub-distributors.

If you were to determine that the site listing your book is a pirate operation, you will have to gather information, or else no one will act on your complaint.

Do a "Who Is" search on the website and identify the owner and the OSP, or Online Service Provider by going to the website http://www.whois.com/ and entering the name of the website that is infringing on your copyright.

You will receive a report on the website in question and within it, you can see the owner's name and physical address, phone number and email address..

The DMCA Notice, or "Digital Millennium Copyright Act Takedown Notice" can be sent to the website. The format for the DMCA Notice is as follows;

Digital Millennium Copyright Act Takedown Notice

My name is _____ and I am the author of the book(s) listed in this DMCA Takedown Notice.

A website that your company hosts (according to WHOIS information) is infringing on at least one copyright owned by me.

A book is available for download from your server without my permission.

The original book, where I own exclusive copyright, can be found at is: http://WWW.xxxxx.com/

The unauthorized and infringing copy can be found at: http://WWW.xxxxx.com/.

This letter is official notification under Section 512(c) of the Digital Millennium Copyright Act ("DMCA"), and I seek the removal of the aforementioned infringing material from your servers. I request that you immediately notify the copyright infringer of this notice and inform them of their duty to remove the infringing material immediately, and notify them to cease any further posting of infringing material to your server in the future.

Please also be advised that the law requires you, as a service provider, to remove or disable access to the infringing materials upon receiving this notice.

Under US law a service provider, such as yourself, enjoys immunity from a copyright lawsuit provided that you act with deliberate speed to investigate and rectify ongoing copyright infringement.

If service providers do not investigate and remove or disable the infringing material this immunity is lost. Therefore, in order for you to remain immune from a copyright infringement action you will need to investigate and speedily remove or otherwise disable the infringing material.

In the event that your client does not comply immediately, the responsibility falls to you.

Under penalty of perjury I certify that the information contained in the notification is both true and accurate, and I have the authority to act as the owner of the copyright(s) involved.

Should you wish to discuss this with me please contact me directly.

Thank you.

YOUR NAME
Address, City, State Zip
Phone, E-mail

Next are the most neglected reporting tools in your toolbox. If you have your books published with online distributors, they are losing money as well.

The general feeling is that the online distributors don't want to get involved in the business of protecting your copyright. That is true.

However, the online distributors do want to get involved with protecting their product base and sales revenues. So offer to help them reduce the financial hemorrhaging caused by piracy.

Online distributors are a busy bunch of people and will not be useful in your attempt to take on the pirate if they have to do anything. You will have to do the primary research and give them the results.

After gathering all of the information, you can notify the online distributors and provide them with the following information;

"Who Is" Data Information

Tech Country: GB

Tech Phone: +4.00000000000 <= phone number of the owner

Tech Email: XXXXXXX@mail.com <= email address of owner

Name Server: NS1.DNSEXIT.COM

Name Server: NS2.DNSEXIT.COM

Name Server: NS3.DNSEXIT.COM

Name Server: NS4.DNSEXIT.COM

DNSSEC: Unsigned
URL of the ICANN WHOIS Data Problem Reporting System: http://wdprs.internic.net/
>>> Last update of WHOIS database: 2013-12-05T08:04:04+04:00 <<<
Registrar: REGTIME LTD.
Whois Server: whois.webnames.ru
Creation Date: 23-OCT-2013
Updated Date: 23-OCT-2013
Expiration Date: 23-OCT-2014
Nameserver: NS1.DNSEXIT.COM
Nameserver: NS2.DNSEXIT.COM
Nameserver: NS3.DNSEXIT.COM
Nameserver: NS4.DNSEXIT.COM
Registry Status: ok
Domain Name: XXXXXXXXXXXX.NET <=IP of Pirate site
Registry Domain ID: 1832164520_DOMAIN_NET-VRSN
Registrar WHOIS Server: whois.regtime.net
Registrar URL: http://www.webnames.ru
Updated Date: 2013-10-23T10:41:37+04:00
Creation Date: 2013-10-23T00:00:00+04:00
Registrar Registration Expiration Date: 2014-10-23T04:00:00+04:00
Registrar: REGTIME LTD.
Registrar IANA ID: 1362
Registrar Abuse Contact: abuse@regtime.net <=REGISTRAR
Registrar Abuse Contact Phone: +7.8463733047
Domain Status: OK
Registry Registrant ID: CO1406492-RT

Registrant Name: David XXXXXX   <=owner name
Registrant Organization: David XXXXX <=owner organization
Registrant Street: 152-153 XXXX St   <=owner street address
Registrant City: London   <=owner city
Registrant State/Province: England   <=owner State & Country
Registrant Postal Code: EC4A2DQ   <=owner Postal Code
Registrant Country: GB
Registrant Phone: +4.XXXXXXXXXXX
Registrant Email: XXXXXXXX@mail.com
Registry Admin ID: CAXXXXXX-RT
Admin Name: David XXXXXX
Admin Organization: David XXXXXX
Admin Street: 152-153 XXXXX St
Admin City: London
Admin State/Province: England
Admin Postal Code: EC4A2DQ
Admin Country: GB
Admin Phone: +4.XXXXXXXXXXX
Admin Email: XXXXXXXX@mail.com
Registry Tech ID: CTXXXXXXX-RT
Tech Name: David XXXXXX
Tech Organization: David XXXXXX
Tech Street: 152-153 XXXX St
Tech City: London
Tech State/Province: England
Tech Postal Code: EC4A2DQ
Tech Country: GB

Tech Phone: +4.XXXXXXXXXXX
Tech Email: XXXXXXXX@mail.com
Name Server: NS1.DNSEXIT.COM
Name Server: NS2.DNSEXIT.COM
Name Server: NS3.DNSEXIT.COM
Name Server: NS4.DNSEXIT.COM
DNSSEC: Unsigned
URL of the ICANN WHOIS Data Problem Reporting System:
http://wdprs.internic.net/
>>> Last update of WHOIS database: 2013-12-05T08:04:04+04:00 <<<
Registrar: REGTIME LTD.
Whois Server: whois.webnames.ru
Creation Date: 23-OCT-2013
Updated Date: 23-OCT-2013
Expiration Date: 23-OCT-2014
Nameserver: NS1.DNSEXIT.COM
Nameserver: NS2.DNSEXIT.COM
Nameserver: NS3.DNSEXIT.COM
Nameserver: NS4.DNSEXIT.COM
Registry Status: ok
TRANSFERRED REGISTRATION TO
Domain Name: XXXXXXXXXXXX.NET
Registrar: REGTIME LTD.
Whois Server: whois.webnames.ru
Referral URL: http://www.webnames.ru
Name Server: NS1.DNSEXIT.COM
Name Server: NS2.DNSEXIT.COM
Name Server: NS3.DNSEXIT.COM
Name Server: NS4.DNSEXIT.COM

Status: ok
Updated Date: 23-Oct-2013
Creation Date: 23-Oct-2013
Expiration Date: 23-Oct-2014

ICANN

The ICANN, or Internet Corporation for Assigned Names and Numbers has a Complaint URL where you can file a complaint. Give them all of your information as they request it.

Make sure they can respond to your complaint and that you are not withhold any information about your identity. They won't take you seriously if you don't identify yourself and your email address.
http://wdprs.internic.net/

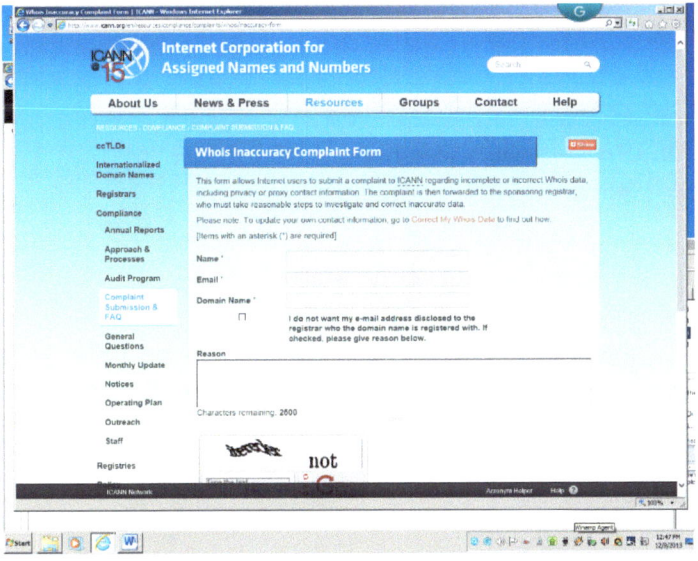

The Main screen for the ICANN complaint department is shown above. Make sure you file an accurate report.

WHAT'S A REGISTRAR?

When you want to own a website, you contact a Registrar and, if the website name is available, you can pay to have the Registrar "host" the site.

In the example of the investigation in this book, the Registrar is Russian. Some people believe that in countries where the law is flaunted, you can't get any satisfaction with regard to the pirating of books. It really doesn't matter what country the Registrar is located in. The ICANN and the DCMA are global and in control.

You can view the 2009 RAA at:

http://www.icann.org/en/registrars/ra-agreement-21may09-en.htm

The address, phone number, and FAX for ICANN is shown below:

Internet Corporation for
Assigned Names and Numbers
12025 Waterfront Drive, Suite 300
Los Angeles, California 90094-2536 USA
Attention: Registrar Relations
Telephone: 310-823-9358
Facsimile: 310-823-8649

Complaints for Registrars are filed by email at the appropriate Registrar. Each Registrar is different.

The complaint email address for the Russian Registrar called RegTime is shown below:

Registrar Abuse Contact: abuse@regtime.net

ICANN currently accredits domain-name registrars for the following Top Level Domains. These suffixes are assigned for the purposes described:

- [.aero](), (reserved for the global aviation community) sponsored by Societe Internationale de Telecommunications Aeronautiques (SITA INC USA)

- [.asia](), (reserved for the Pan-Asia and Asia Pacific region) sponsored by DotAsia Organisation

- [.biz](), (restricted to businesses), operated by NeuStar, Inc.

- [.cat](), (reserved for the Catalan linguistic and cultural community), sponsored by Fundació puntCat.

- [.com](), operated by VeriSign, Inc.

- [.coop](), (reserved for cooperatives) sponsored by Dot Cooperation LLC

- [.info](), operated by Afilias Limited

- **.jobs**, (reserved for the human resource management community) sponsored by Employ Media LLC

- **.mobi**, (reserved for consumers and providers of mobile products and services) sponsored by mTLD Top Level Domain, Ltd.

- **.museum**, (restricted to museums and related persons), sponsored by the Museum Domain Management Association International (MDI)

- **.name**, (restricted to individuals), operated by Verisign Information Services, Inc.

- **.net**, operated by VeriSign, Inc.

- **.org**, operated by Public Interest Registry

- **.pro**, (restricted to licensed professionals) operated by Registry Services Corporation (dba RegistryPro)

- **.tel**, (reserved for individuals and businesses to store and manage their contact information in the DNS) sponsored by Telnic Limited

- **.travel**, (reserved for entities whose primary area of activity is in the travel industry) sponsored by Tralliance Registry Management Company, LLC

- **.xxx**, (reserved for online adult entertainment) sponsored by ICM Registry, LLC

The following company has been accredited by ICANN to act as a registrar in one or more TLDs. The version of the RAA (Registrar Accreditation Agreement) indicated after each registrar name designates which contract they have signed with ICANN. The 2009 RAA indicates that the registrar has signed the 2009 Registrar Accreditation Agreement, which provides enhanced protections for registrants and an increased level of accountability for registrars.

The 2001 RAA is an older contract with fewer protections. Prospective registrants may want to take this fact into account when selecting a registrar for their gTLD name(s).

The RAA version is not an indication of how long the registrar has been ICANN accredited.

CHAPTER 13 THE MAILING LIST

Mailing lists are often found on the Internet. I have happened across some interesting mailing lists on search engines.

Chambers of commerce often have a list of their members available to those who wish to do business with the members. It works two ways.

Find these businesses and add them to your mailing list. Be very careful not to alienate the potential customer with SPAM or Junk Mail.

Contacting them one-by-one is the best way to get them on your list. First have a discussion with them about who you are and what you are doing.

CHAPTER 14 GOOD OLD EXCEL

What used to take hours of pencil work with "green-bar" paper and a calculator is totally automated by using good old Microsoft Excel.

CHAPTER 15 GETTING YOUR WEBSITE

You can get your website already encoded from Rob Stetson online. Send email or call the number on the main page. If there is no answer, leave a message for a return call.

$ 49.95 by PayPal is accepted for payment.

You will receive a software code for the download of the compressed website which can be unzipped and does not require installation.

The unzipped website was created using a Mozzila HTML web page editor, Your pages will require configuration using a web page editor such as Mozzila.

Mouse over Menus can be edited using Menu Maker by Xara Group Ltd. This software will enable you to edit, add or delete menu buttons easily.

The custom pages can be pre-configured to your requirements for a fee. Product web links and custom Internet links are done for a fee. Your photo and custom text on web pages are done for a fee.

Strange or complex custom configurations may not be available. The configuration platform offered is like the one seen in this book along with security buttons and pages.

The power of a web site is enormous, giving you credibility and directing people to other websites where they can buy your books.

At the risk of sounding like a sales pitch, you only need one or two pages to start. It's really cheap to set up (I can do it for you) and it gives people a place to go where you have no competition while showing all you have to offer.

One example of a **free page** is shown here. I set this up on Lulu.com. It features almost all of my books in one place with one click. Yes, it is actually free.

http://www.lulu.com/spotlight/RobStetson?searchTerms=&pageOffset=1

If you want to see what a personal website looks like, try this link;

http://www.RobStetson.com

Other menu items can let people know a little about you so they can get a flavor for just who you are.

The website is a target for the free business card sized brochures in chapter 1; otherwise it will only get the traffic you send that way.

Making HTML WEB PAGES

You're going to be doing a lot of linking to the Internet in order to make your Web Site. I just thought I'd say a few words to help you get the job done in case you decide to do it yourself.

The Mozilla HTML editor is my editor of choice. It was a FREE DOWNLOAD that was abandoned by and no longer supported by Mozilla.org, but it works so well I continue to use it. Warnings about the potential security risks haven't been a problem. You can use the editor (recommended) or you can substitute an editor of your own.

Use this editor at your own risk as I can't warrant the safety or effectiveness of this application. It works well, and has continued to work well for me for many years.

If you like the software you can log onto Mozilla.org and make a donation to the non-profit free-software company. Like Firefox and other products,

You can download them and run them at no charge. You can find the link to join Mozilla and make a donation to their company.

Making HTML pages is not as difficult as it might seem.

You start out by opening the HTML editor and typing in the information. To start with, go to; http://www.robstetson.com/addons/mozilla.exe

If you have trouble getting the program to run, right click on the Mozilla icon and then click on the "Properties" option at the bottom of the list. When the option box opens, click on the "General" tab and then near the bottom of the list, click on the box for "Run as an Administrator" and then save. The program should open and run OK now when you click on the icon.

Now double click on the icon and it should open. No upgrades are needed, nor are any upgrades available. This is the latest version of this program, so ignore the message telling you to upgrade, so proceed as though the window is empty.

When the window opens, along the top of the Mozilla window there are a number of options to choose from. This screen IS NOT the editor.

Click on the drop down menu item called "Window" and then click on the list item "Composer" as shown in the screen shot below.

When you click on the menu item called "Composer" as shown above, the window shown below, called the Composer, IS THE EDITOR.

Now you're ready to either load up your HTML file for editing or open a NEW FILE. Click on the drop down menu item called "File" and select "Open File" or New File.

When you have selected a drive location, a directory location and a file name, the Composer will open the HTML file for editing.

Now you can start filling out the page with your photos, if you desire, and your text.

Let's take a look at the Menu Maker software.

For less than $ 20 you can have the beauty of mouse over menus for your website. These menus are impressive and you have a variety of different styles to choose from. These menus can be run along the top or down the side of the page.

For a website, I recommend having them down the left side of the page. This magical menu software can be purchased from Xara Group Ltd.

The link to obtain this software is

http://www.creationengine.com/html/p.lasso?l=Xara%20Menu%20Maker&p=13551

DIRECT SELL YOUR EBOOKS OFFLINE

In the spirit of keeping this book on track I want to tell you that you don't have to buy this software. You can create menus that work perfectly well by using "Links".

To use Links to build a menu, just type the word you want to use as a menu item and then highlight it and click on "INSERT" and "LINK". Type in the location of the item and you have a menu item.

Let's take a short tour of this Xara Menu Software so you can decide whether or not this is the way to go.

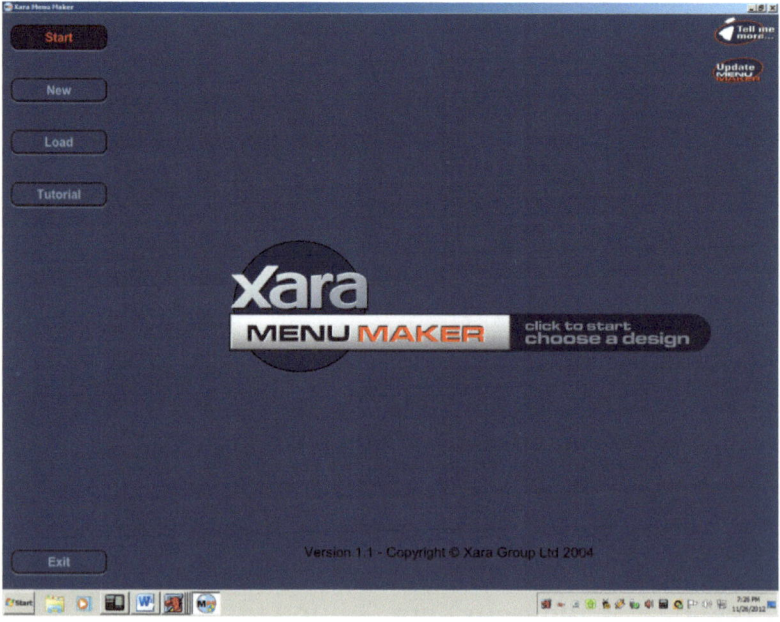

The software opens with this main page. Every time you open the software it checks automatically for upgrades, so you might get a page informing you as to whether or not there are upgrades to install. I notice that if you're in and out of the program several times in a short period, it doesn't bother you with the upgrade info screen.

Notice the buttons on the left called "START", "NEW", "LOAD", and "TUTORIAL".

If you have a menu that you have been working on, it will automatically load when you click on START.

START. This is the starting point for your first Menu. Notice that the second layer menu extends out to the right when you put the mouse on the buttons that have sub-menus available.

DESIGNS. The button opens the button style page.

Notice too that there are nineteen pages of button styles that you can wade through until you find one that you like. You can select the colors for the menu items on the list, and you can select the color of the sub-menu. From the perspective of color, you can have any combination of colors to mark the two states. One static state is the "Mouse" state where the mouse is not touching the button. The "Active" state is when the mouse pointer, or index, is placed on the button.

The designs page is for selecting the menu button design and the texture of the background.

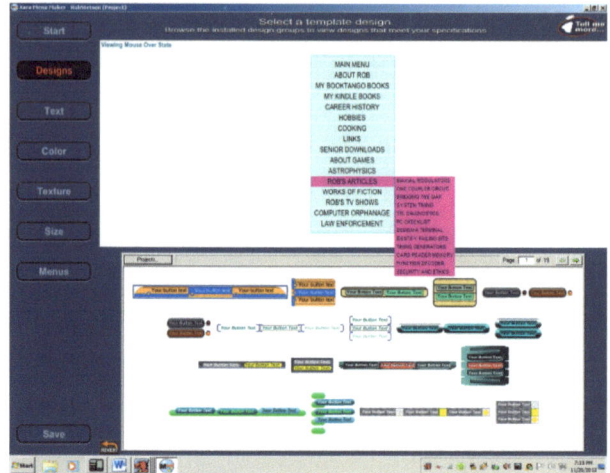

The page above is the button design page. Before you even begin to develop a menu, you pick the appearance of your menu buttons, their size and color. The menu appearance is completely flexible.

Even at this late juncture in the menu development stage, you can change the menu design and colors.

TEXT. The page below is for selecting the font, size and style of the writing on the menus. Notice the wide array of fonts and styles in the text control box.

DIRECT SELL YOUR EBOOKS OFFLINE

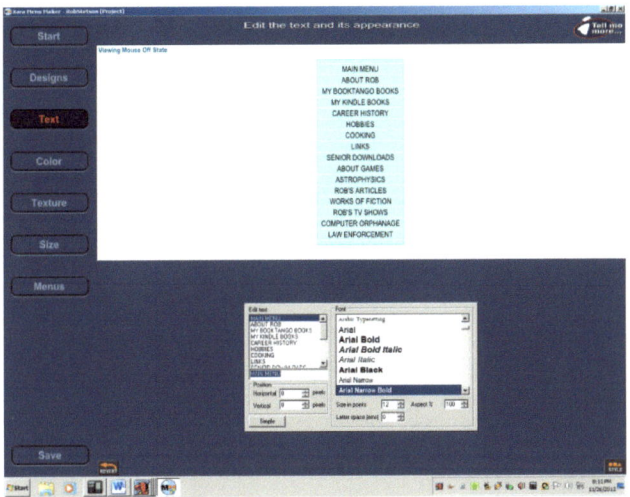

Here again, the font size, style and appearance in the screen shot shown above is not just determined at the outset of the menu design, but can be changed at any time after the menu is fully developed and functional.

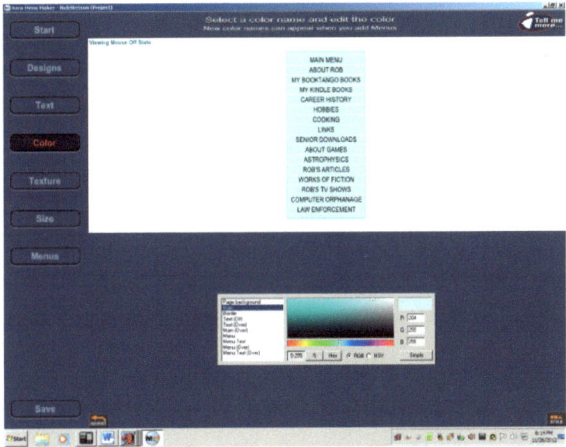

COLOR. The Color button shown in the screen shot above enables you to change the color of the text, and the buttons color for both the static state and the mouse over state. The sub-menus have the same color flexibility as the main menu.

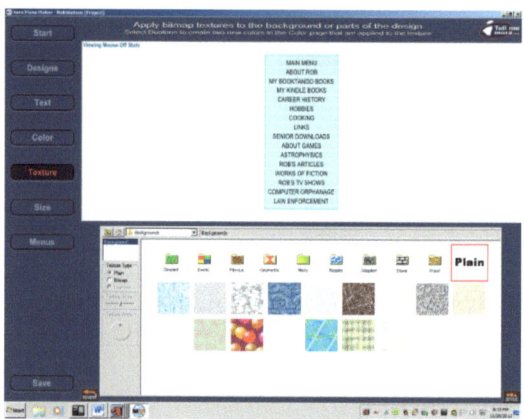

TEXTURE. The background texture is under your control with the texture button. You can make distinctive backgrounds with the click of a mouse. The banner shown on the top of the last index.htm screen shot shown in Chapter 2 that says, "Constable Stetson" and "Getting the job done" was made using the texture button here. I had selected the block 8 boxes to the right called "Stone" as a background. Then I put the title (Constable Stetson) in a big blue box and overlaid it with a smaller white box (Getting the job done) to give an artful appearance.

Enough of the stone background shows around the perimeter of the boxes to make the sign look good. You can use the texture button anywhere you have a data, art or photo field to make the background set a basic platform for the content..

Just a suggestion here, but go lightly with all the special effects when you're making a Web Site because too many special effects can make the entire appearance look bad. A little goes a long way here.

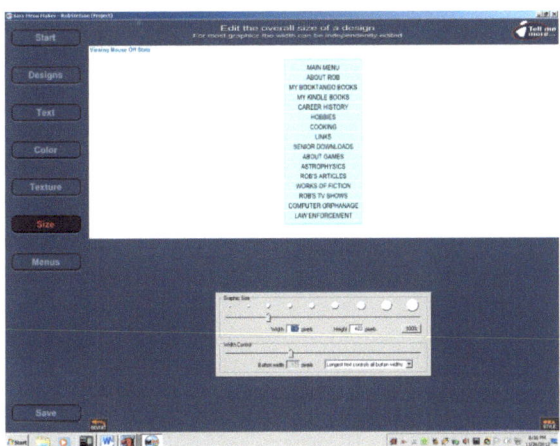

SIZE. Shown in the screen shot shown above. The size, spacing and overall positioning of the fonts on the menu buttons can be adjusted to give the menu buttons that finished look.

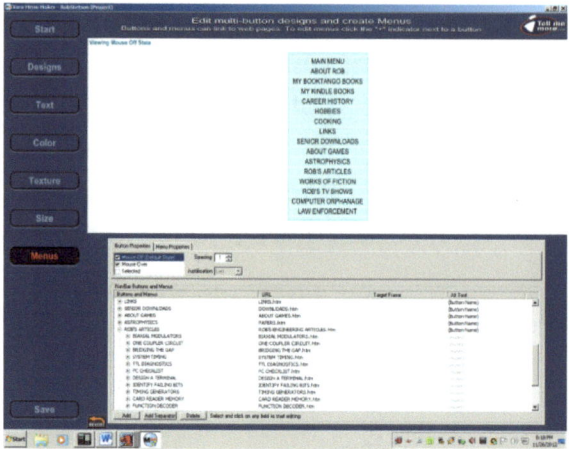

MENUS. Menu contents, file names and their extensions are shown in the screen shot above. Here you can create menu buttons, their function, their submenu names and functions, etc.

You can not only create the buttons and drop down submenus, but you can delete the ones you don't want. This makes the entire menu structure dynamic even after the menu has been completed and in use for a period of time. It can always be modified.

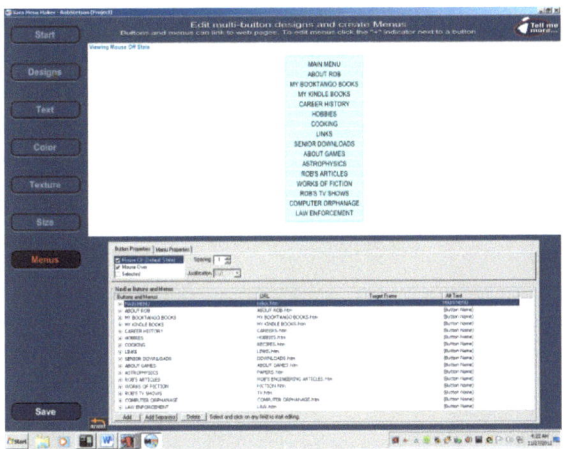

SAVE. That Save button in the screen shot shown above in the lower left hand corner is your opportunity to save the project and then create the menu in your HTML pages.

The Menu is saved as a Java Script and is reflected in all of the pages in your website. You only have to create the menu once and then it propagates throughout the project.

It's a good idea to create your menu early on for the project and then add to it as you expand your pages. Always test as you go, because once you have a significant number of pages, problem pages will be harder to locate.

The Save button will be the most difficult button to master because it sends you to the areas where you have to decide where the menu goes and whether or not to overwrite existing menu buttons.

Any time you make a change you will have to overwrite your previous menu information, in case you made changes to those selections.

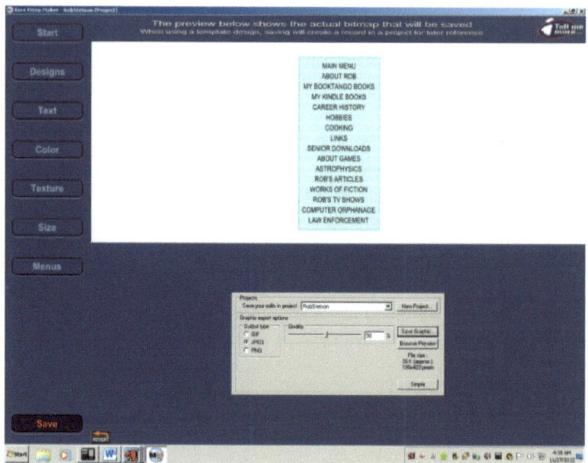

When you click on the save button it opens a box labeled Projects where you have a drop down menu with your project names listed.

The default name appears in the window, but if you choose to, you can save it under a different existing project name.

You can assign a new project name by clicking on the "New Project" button, which will open a new folder and save the project under a new name that you will be asked to assign.

The "Quality slide" is a control for the resolution of the buttons, but be careful with assigning too high a quality to the menu. It will slow down the loading of the menu.

On the left, there are three radio buttons where you can select the format for the graphics. You can choose between ".GIF", ".JPG" or ".PNG" formats. I generally prefer the ".JPG" format because it's the most universal format of them all.

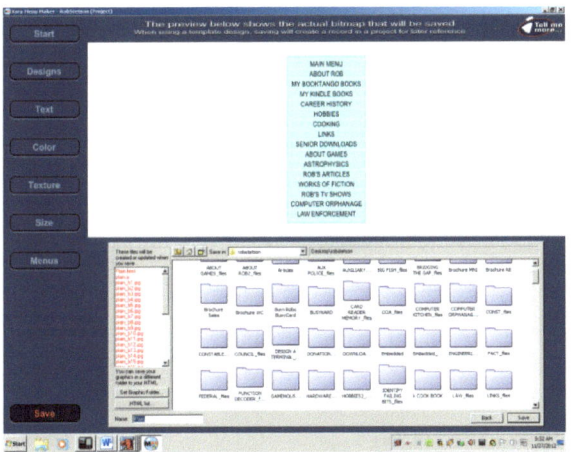

The screen shot above is the result of clicking on the "Save Graphic" button. The box on the left is a list of the button files and Java script to be saved in the "Save In" directory named in the drop down menu at the top of the window. You can elect to save the menu in the first directory you worked in, or designate a new directory.

The List of Java files is red if the file already exists in the named directory. You will have to overwrite any menu files already in the directory if you want to save any changes to any part of it.

Under the list of graphic files there is a set graphic folder button and tucked under all of these entries in the bottom left hand corner is the JPEG file names to be assigned to the buttons.

This gives you the option of having more than one menu on a page.

DIRECT SELL YOUR EBOOKS OFFLINE

On the lower right hand side of the window are the "Back" and "Save" buttons. Back lets you go back and make changes to the previous entries and the Save button finalizes your changes to the menu in the HTML pages.

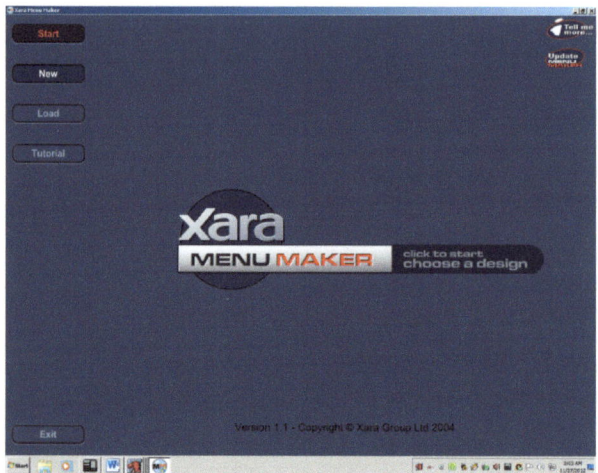

NEW. The "New" button shown above allows you to create a new folder any time you want. When you click on the New Button, it opens up a screen like the one shown below, where you can either add a whole new project to the list or select from a list of either current or past projects. The project selection screen is shown in the screen shot below.

125

DIRECT SELL YOUR EBOOKS OFFLINE

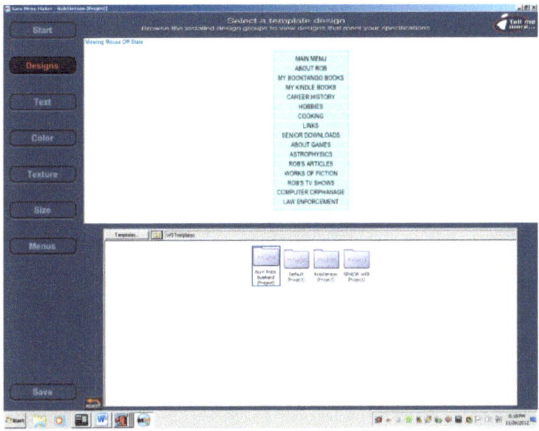

For the rest of the buttons down the left side of the main screen in the screen shot shown above, TEXT through MENUS are the same as they were for the "NEW" button when selected on the main screen.

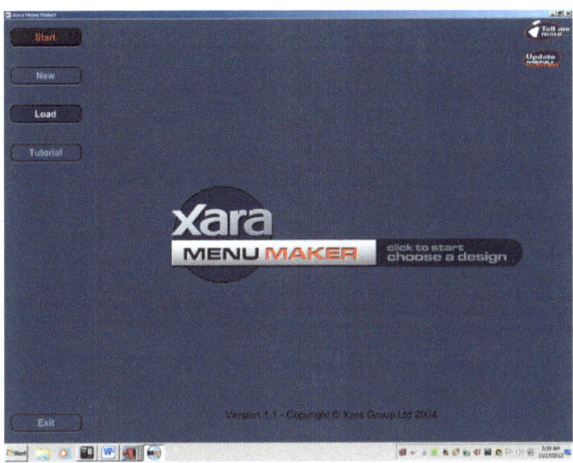

LOAD. The Load function shown in the screen shot above serves the same general purpose as the New button did when you made your first

DIRECT SELL YOUR EBOOKS OFFLINE

menu. If there were no New button, and there were no menus to Load, then you couldn't have started making menus. So the New button is only used once to start your projects.

From here on you will be using the Load button to change menu projects, otherwise, when you start the Menu Maker software it will automatically load and present you with the last project you worked on. This keeps you from having to constantly use the Load button every time you go back into the program when you are trying to complete a project.

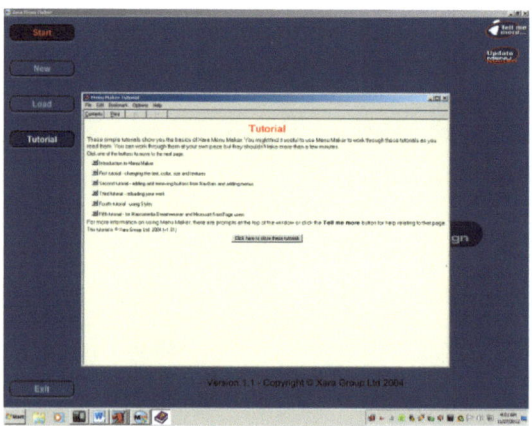

TUTORIAL. The Tutorial button shown in the screen shot above gives you the help menu for a variety of functions in case you have a question regarding the software or its functionality.

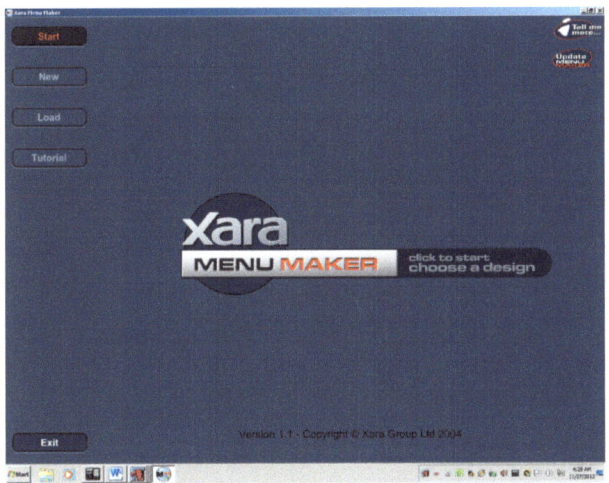

EXIT. **That good old Exit button located in the lower left hand corner of the screen shot shown above allows for a graceful exit from the program. Always exit the program with the exit button. It's frustrating to spend half a day building your menu only to lose it all because you shut down without saving your changes.**

I recommend it for building and maintaining all of your HTML pages in all of your applications. It's only $ 20 and it does a great job. It's easy to use too.

MAKING LINK MENUS

You can save the $ 20 for Xara Menu Maker by using standard links to build a menu. It's more labor intensive and you don't have the option of creating drop down sub-menus.

I actually use a combination of Xara Menus and Links on my pages. An example of this is the Kindle Books page of my Web Site shown below.

Links are a variety of different lengths and even if you try to stack them, the wide variety of lengths will make it difficult to create a neat appearance on the page.

Another design approach would be to click on book cover photos.

FULL COLOR PHOTOS

Your website can take on the aura of a fine magazine with your photo arrangement.

Your website is your company's business card. While the competition is handing out the salesman's personal contact card, you will be handing out a full blown, in depth card featuring your contact information on the label, your company's features and benefits along with any product information.

When everyone has returned to their office, your competition will have to follow up just to remind the potential client of their products and services. You will follow up as well, but the potential client has everything you need to tell them in their hand.

Your competition will be writing letters and mailing out brochures to sell themselves. Long before their literature arrives and is tossed out as junk mail, your sales information will have been in the potential clients' hands.

The paper gets dumped in the trash, but Business Cards are kept, which means they will be keeping everything you want them to know about you and your company. Also, if you are using your web site, you can easily change the information accessed.

The HTML code for inserting a photo is pretty straight forward, but you don't have to know how to insert the code because the Mozilla program makes it as easy as "drag and drop".

The code required for the photo insertion is shown below.

```
<img src="Stet1.jpg" alt="" style="width: 216px; height: 271px;"><br>
```

The following breakdown below explains the code content.

The code content "img" defines the type of HTML entry.

The code content src="Stet1.jpg" is the picture file name.

The code content alt="" is alternative text for unsupported file types.

The code content style="width: 216px; is the photo width in pixels.

The code content height: 271px;" is the photo height in pixels.

The code content <br> is a new line command at the end of the line.

INSERTING ACTION VIDEOS

Whether cartoons, video tours of your business location, commercial messages or personal sales presentation on video, you can dazzle the potential customer.

If you can record a video with sound in "AVI", "VCD", "DV", or "DVD" then your website can play them on the potential customer's computers.

Your entire "dog and pony show" will be seen by the customer immediately.

The HTML code for inserting a full color video with sound is shown below.

`<a ref="Fireworks.wmv">Fireworks</a><br>`

The alternate text is fireworks.

With so many supported video streams available, you can pull out the old camera and cut yourself a lot of advertising with little or no cost. The cost of distribution to your exact demographic is 100%. You won't find that kind of market penetration with any other medium.

Business cards are not usually declined, whereas brochures and other advertising are commonly rejected.

The website becomes somewhat of a wolf in sheep's clothing (I wanted to say a Trojan horse, but that has negative connotations).

INSERTING SOUND BITES

Sound bites are easy to integrate into your pages. The following HTML code will play a song while the customer looks over the menu to decide which area to visit.

```
<embed src="stranger.mp3" hidden="true" loop="FALSE" autostart="TRUE">
```

The code content, embed indicates that the sound file is embedded.

The code content src="stranger.mp3" is the name of the file.

The code content hidden="true", the command to play is invisible.

The code content loop="FALSE" The song plays once. Does not loop.

The code content

autostart="TRUE"

The song plays automatically.

The song played by this string in my website is a relaxing instrumental called "Stranger on the Shore".

MAKE WEB LINKS

Your website can link directly and seamlessly to the Internet in order to provide enormous multipage presentations and catalogs. Your potential customer can visit your web site, tour your factory via video with sound presentations and listen to you as you sit or stand and address them as though you were in their office.

Your menu buttons can put them in your brochure, web site or any other place around the world and it will appear as though they were still looking at the website content.

A DOWNLOAD PLACE

Instructions for installing the code is located on the web at;

http://robstetson.com/password code.doc

The code is installed on your HTML web page using the HTML Editor to cut and paste the code from the document to your page code.

The use of passwords can allow your web site to perform many functions.

If you want to build these barriers into your BusyKard and your website, then here is the public domain code.

I have left the website address and the credit to Joe Barta for having created this public domain program. His website is gone, abandoned, after the passing of all these 10 years, but the public domain code works just fine.

Follow the 4 steps and you will have secure pages.

The following is a copy of the information contained in the web document.

Step 1: Save this image onto your hard drive:

Step 2: Copy the following into the <body> tags of the starting page (The page before the password protected one).

```
<SCRIPT LANGUAGE="javascript">
<!--- Hide from tired old browsers
var nifty_little_window = null;
function gateKeeper() {
nifty_little_window = window.open('gatekeep.html', 'theKeeper',
'width=350,height=200,resizable=1');
}
// End hiding --->
</SCRIPT>
<form>
```

```
<input type="button" value="Enter Here" onClick="gateKeeper()"
</form>
```

Step 3: Copy this and save it as a new page. Save it as "gatekeep.html"

```
<HTML>
<HEAD>
<TITLE>Gate Keeper</TITLE>
<SCRIPT LANGUAGE="JavaScript">
<!--- Hide from tired old browsers that should be put to pasture.
//////////////////////////////////////////////////////////
/// Get your very own Gate Keeper from Professional Web Design ///
///
http://junior.apk.net/~jbarta/weblinks/gate_keeper/
///
//////////////////////////////////////////////////////////
function goForit() {
 var location;
 var password;
 password=this.document.testform.inputbox.value
 location=password + ".html"
 fetch(location)
 theKeeper=window.close()
}
function fetch(location) {
 var root;
 if (opener.closed) {

root=window.open('','theKeepersGopher','toolbar=yes,
```

```
location=yes,status=yes,menubar=yes,scrollbars=yes
,resizable=yes,copyhistory=no');
    root.location.href = location;
  } else {
   opener.location.href = location;
  }
 }
 // End hiding --->
 </SCRIPT>
 </HEAD>
 <BODY BACKGROUND="keeper.gif">
 <TABLE BORDER=0 CELLPADDING=0
CELLSPACING=0 WIDTH=100%>
 <TR>
 <TD ROWSPAN=2 WIDTH=50%>
  
 <TD WIDTH=50% ALIGN=CENTER
VALIGN=MIDDLE>
 <FONT FACE="ARIAL" SIZE=2><B>Hold on there
buddy. You'll need a password to get in here. We're
tryin' to keep out the riff-raff.</B></FONT><BR>
  
 <TR>
 <TD WIDTH=50% ALIGN=CENTER
VALIGN=BOTTOM>
  <CENTER>
  <FORM NAME="testform">
  <INPUT TYPE="text" NAME="inputbox" VALUE=""
size=20>
```

```
    <INPUT TYPE="button" NAME="button"
Value="Submit Password"
onClick="goForit(this.form)">
    ///<!--- You can remove the following link if you
want.
    ///   I just added it to satisfy my own selfish
interests.
    ///   Just remove the following line and this
comment. --->
    ///<P><FONT SIZE=1 FACE="COMIC SANS
MS"><A
///HREF="http://junior.apk.net/~jbarta/weblinks/gate_k
eeper/
  " TARGET="_blank"><B>Gate
Keeper</B></A></FONT>
    </FORM>
    </CENTER>
    </TABLE>
    </BODY>
    </HTML>
```

Step 4 (final one):

You're basically done. The above will password protect any page, the password being the name of the file. For example, say I want to protect mypage.htm. The password would be "mypage". So all you have to do now is rename the page you want to protect to a longer and more complicated file name, and that will be the password that will access that page. No, you don't have to add anything to the protected page.

Note: It seems this script can only protect pages that end in ".html", and NOT ".htm", so be sure to rename the extensions too.

Please realize again that this script is written by Joe Barta, a talented webmaster.

ABOUT USING SECURE AREAS

One of the attributes that make the password protection such a miraculous thing is the ability to filter what the holder has access to.

As you hand your "download authorization cards" out to people, whether vendors or customers, you can write the password on the card's label with a felt tip pen.

As people use the card, they will enter parts of the web site that are password protected and see only the information intended for them, such as the book waiting for them to download and install it.

As you see the areas open to various select people, bear in mind that it doesn't just open a new area.

Password protection can actually cause whole new menus and options to appear. It's like having several individual, unique web sites, along with several individual, unique menus, all wrapped up in one.

You can have your catalog, contact information and phone numbers for all to see, This way anyone wanting your product will be in command of the pricing and product information.

It opens a window for your customers to see your inventory and retail pricing along with product availability. You can include preferred pricing for preferred customers, invisible to people who are not "preferred" buyers. You decide what each class of customer sees. Meanwhile, non-preferred customers will see their pricing as the only pricing available.

www.ingramcontent.com/pod-product-compliance
Lightning Source LLC
Chambersburg PA
CBHW040806200526
45159CB00022B/25